Platform Capitalism

Theory Redux

Series editor: Laurent de Sutter

Platform Capitalism

Nick Srnicek

polity

First published in 2017 by Polity Press

Polity Press
65 Bridge Street
Cambridge CB2 1UR, UK

Polity Press
350 Main Street
Malden, MA 02148, USA

ISBN-13: 978-1-5095-0486-2
ISBN-13: 978-1-5095-0487-9(pb)

A catalogue record for this book is available from the British Library.

Library of Congress Cataloging-in-Publication Data

Names: Srnicek, Nick, author. | De Sutter, Laurent, author.
Title: Platform capitalism / Nick Srnicek, Laurent de Sutter.
Description: Cambridge, UK ; Malden, MA : Polity Press, 2016. | Series:
Theory redux | Includes bibliographical references.
Identifiers: LCCN 2016023187 (print) | LCCN 2016036308 (ebook) | ISBN
9781509504862 (hardback) | ISBN 9781509504879 (pbk.) | ISBN 9781509504893
(Mobi) | ISBN 9781509504909 (Epub)
Subjects: LCSH: Information technology--Economic aspects. | Business
enterprises. | Multi-sided platform businesses. | Capitalism--History.
Classification: LCC HC79.I55 .S685 2016 (print) | LCC HC79.I55 (ebook) | DDC
330.12/209--dc23
LC record available at https://lccn.loc.gov/2016023187

Typeset in 12.5 on 15 pt Adobe Garamond by
Servis Filmsetting Ltd, Stockport, Cheshire
Printed and bound in Great Britain by CPI Group (UK) Ltd, Croydon

Contents

Acknowledgements

A number of people have helped to bring this book to fruition. Thanks to Laurent de Sutter for initiating the project and to the team at Polity for bringing it all together – George Owers, Neil de Cort, and Manuela Tecusan. Alex Andrews was an immensely helpful technical advisor, and thanks to everyone else who read earlier drafts – Diann Bauer, Suhail Malik, Benedict Singleton, Keith Tilford, Alex Williams, and two anonymous reviewers. Last but not least, thanks to Helen Hester for supporting me and for always being my most intellectually challenging and insightful critic.

Introduction

We are told today that we are living in an age of massive transformation. Terms like the sharing economy, the gig economy, and the fourth industrial revolution are tossed around, with enticing images of entrepreneurial spirit and flexibility bandied about. As workers, we are to be liberated from the constraints of a permanent career and given the opportunity to make our own way by selling whatever goods and services we might like to offer. As consumers, we are presented with a cornucopia of on-demand services and with the promise of a network of connected devices that cater to our every whim. This is a book on this contemporary moment and its avatars in emerging technologies: platforms, big data, additive manufacturing, advanced robotics, machine learning, and the internet of things. It is not the first book to look at these topics, but it takes a different approach from others. In the existing literature, one group of commentaries focuses on the politics of emerging technology, emphasising privacy and state surveillance but leaving aside economic issues around ownership and profitability. Another group looks at how corporations are embodiments of particular ideas and values and criticises them for not acting humanely – but, again, it neglects the economic context and the imperatives of a capitalist system.[1] Other scholars do examine these emerging economic trends but present them as sui generis phenomena, disconnected from their history. They never ask why we have this economy today, nor do they recognise how today's economy responds to yesterday's problems. Finally, a number of analyses report on how poor the smart economy is for workers and how digital labour represents a shift in the relationship between workers and capital, but they leave aside any analysis of broader economic trends and intercapitalist competition.[2]

The present book aims to supplement these other perspectives by giving an economic history of capitalism and digital technology, while recognising the diversity of economic forms and the competitive tensions inherent in the contemporary economy. The simple wager of the book is that we can learn a lot about major tech companies by taking them to be economic actors within a capitalist mode of production. This means abstracting from them as cultural actors defined by the values of the Californian ideology, or as political actors seeking to wield power. By contrast, these actors are compelled to seek out profits in order to fend off competition. This places strict limits on what constitutes possible and predictable expectations of what is likely to occur. Most notably, capitalism demands that firms constantly seek out new avenues for profit, new markets, new commodities, and new means of exploitation. For some, this focus on capital rather than labour may suggest a vulgar economism; but, in a world where the labour movement has been significantly weakened, giving capital a priority of agency seems only to reflect reality.

Where, then, do we focus our attention if we wish to see the effects of digital technology on capitalism? We might turn to the technology sector,[3] but, strictly speaking, this sector remains a relatively small part of the economy. In the United States it currently contributes around 6.8 per cent of the value added from private companies and employs about 2.5 per cent of the labour force.[4] By comparison, manufacturing in the deindustrialised United States employs four times as many people. In the United Kingdom manufacturing employs nearly three times as many people as the tech sector.[5] This is in part because tech companies are notoriously small. Google has around 60,000 direct employees, Facebook has 12,000, while WhatsApp had 55 employees when it was sold to Facebook for $19 billion and Instagram had 13 when it was purchased for $1 billion. By comparison, in 1962 the most significant companies employed far larger numbers of workers: AT&T had 564,000 employees, Exxon had 150,000 workers, and GM had 605,000 employees.[6] Thus, when we discuss the digital economy, we should bear in mind that it is something broader than just the tech sector defined according to standard classifications.

As a preliminary definition, we can say that the digital economy refers to those businesses that increasingly rely upon information technology, data, and the internet for their business models.

This is an area that cuts across traditional sectors – including manufacturing, services, transportation, mining, and telecommunications – and is in fact becoming essential to much of the economy today. Understood in this way, the digital economy is far more important than a simple sectoral analysis might suggest. In the first place, it appears to be the most dynamic sector of the contemporary economy – an area from which constant innovation is purportedly emerging and that seems to be guiding economic growth forward. The digital economy appears to be a leading light in an otherwise rather stagnant economic context. Secondly, digital technology is becoming systematically important, much in the same way as finance. As the digital economy is an increasingly pervasive infrastructure for the contemporary economy, its collapse would be economically devastating. Lastly, because of its dynamism, the digital economy is presented as an ideal that can legitimate contemporary capitalism more broadly. The digital economy is becoming a hegemonic model: cities are to become smart, businesses must be disruptive, workers are to become flexible, and governments must be lean and intelligent. In this environment those who work hard can take advantage of the changes and win out. Or so we are told.

The argument of this book is that, with a long decline in manufacturing profitability, capitalism has turned to data as one way to maintain economic growth and vitality in the face of a sluggish production sector. In the twenty-first century, on the basis of changes in digital technologies, data have become increasingly central to firms and their relations with workers, customers, and other capitalists. The platform has emerged as a new business model, capable of extracting and controlling immense amounts of data, and with this shift we have seen the rise of large monopolistic firms. Today the capitalism of the high- and middle-income economies is increasingly dominated by these firms, and the dynamics outlined in this book suggest that the trend is only going to continue. The aim here is to set these platforms in the context of a larger economic history, understand them as means to generate profit, and outline some of the tendencies they produce as a result.

In part, this book is a synthesis of existing work. The discussion in Chapter 1 should be familiar to economic historians, as it outlines the various crises that have laid the groundwork for today's post-2008 economy. It attempts to historicise emerging technologies as an outcome of deeper capitalist tendencies, showing how they are implicated within a system of exploitation, exclusion, and competition. The material in Chapter 2 should be fairly well known to those who follow the business of technology. In many ways, the chapter is an attempt to give clarity to various ongoing discussions in that world, as it lays out a typology and genesis of platforms. By contrast, Chapter 3 hopefully offers something new to everyone. On the basis of the preceding chapters, it attempts to draw out some likely tendencies and to make some broad-brush predictions about the future of platform capitalism. These forward-looking prognoses are essential to any political project. How we conceptualise the past and the future is important for how we think strategically and develop political tactics to transform society today. In short, it makes a difference whether we see emerging technologies as inaugurating a new regime of accumulation or as continuing earlier regimes. This has consequences on the possibility of a crisis and on deciding where that crisis might emerge from; and it has consequences on our envisaging the likely future of labour under capitalism. Part of the argument of this book is that the apparent novelties of the situation obscure the persistence of longer term trends, but also that today presents important changes that must be grasped by a twenty-first-century left. Understanding our position in a broader context is the first step to creating strategies for transforming it.

The Long Downturn

To understand our contemporary situation, it is necessary to see how it links in with what preceded it. Phenomena that appear to be radical novelties may, in historical light, reveal themselves to be simple continuities. In this chapter I will argue that there are three moments in the relatively recent history of capitalism that are particularly relevant to the current conjuncture: the response to the 1970s downturn; the boom and bust of the 1990s; and the response to the 2008 crisis. Each of these moments has set the stage for the new digital economy and has determined the ways in which it has developed. All of this must first be set in the context of our broad economic system of capitalism and of the imperatives and constraints it imposes upon enterprises and workers. While capitalism is an incredibly flexible system, it also has certain invariant features, which function as broad parameters for any given historical period. If we are to understand the causes, dynamics, and consequences of today's situation, we must first understand how capitalism operates.

Capitalism, uniquely among all modes of production to date, is immensely successful at raising productivity levels.[1] This is the key dynamic that expresses capitalist economies' unprecedented capacity to grow at a rapid pace and to raise living standards. What makes capitalism different?[2] This cannot be explained through psychological mechanisms, as though at some time we collectively decided to become greedier or more efficient at producing than our ancestors did. Instead, what explains capitalism's productivity growth is a change in social relationships, particularly property relationships. In precapitalist societies, producers had direct access to their means of subsistence: land for farming and housing. Under those conditions, survival did not systematically depend on how efficiently one's production process was. The vagaries of natural cycles may mean that a crop did not grow at adequate levels for one year, but these were contingent constraints rather than systemic ones. Working sufficiently hard to gain the resources necessary for survival was all that was needed. Under capitalism, this changes. Economic agents are now separated from the means of subsistence and, in order to secure the goods they need for survival, they must now turn to the market. While markets had existed for thousands of years, under capitalism economic agents were uniquely faced with *generalised* market dependence. Production therefore became oriented towards the market: one had to sell goods in order to make the money needed for purchasing subsistence goods. But, as vast numbers of people were now relying upon selling on the market, producers faced competitive pressures. If too costly, their goods would not sell, and they would quickly face the collapse of their business. As a result, generalised market dependency led to a systemic imperative to reduce production costs in relation to prices. This can be done in a variety of ways; but the most significant methods were the adoption of efficient technologies and techniques in the labour process, specialisation, and the sabotage of competitors. The outcome of these competitive actions was eventually expressed in the medium-term tendencies of capitalism: prices tangentially declined to the level of costs, profits across different industries tended to become equal, and relentless growth imposed itself as the ultimate logic of capitalism. This logic of accumulation became an implicit and taken-for-granted element embedded within every business decision: whom to hire, where to invest, what to build, what to produce, who to sell to, and so on.

One of the most important consequences of this schematic model of capitalism is that it demands constant technological change. In the effort to cut costs, beat out competitors, control workers, reduce turnover time, and gain market share, capitalists are incentivised to continually transform the labour process. This was the source of capitalism's immense dynamism, as capitalists tend to increase labour productivity constantly and to outdo one another in generating profits efficiently. But technology is also central to capitalism for other reasons, which we will examine in more detail later on. It has often been used to deskill workers and undermine the power of skilled labourers (though there are countertendencies towards reskilling as well).[3] These deskilling technologies enable cheaper and more pliable workers to come in and replace the skilled ones, as well as transferring the mental processes of work to management rather than leaving it in the hands of workers on the shop floor. Behind these technical changes, however, lies competition and struggle – both between classes, in their struggle to gain strength at one another's expense, and between capitalists, in their efforts to lower the costs of production below the social average. It is the latter dynamic, in particular, that will play a key role in the changes that lie at heart of this book. But before we can understand the digital economy we must look back to an earlier period.

The End of the Postwar Exception

It is increasingly obvious to many that we live in a time still coming to terms with the breakdown of the postwar settlement. Thomas Piketty argues that the reduction in inequality after the Second World War was an exception to the general rule of capitalism; Robert Gordon sees high productivity growth in the middle of the twentieth century as an exception to the historical norm; and numerous thinkers on the left have long argued that the postwar period was an unsustainably good period for capitalism.[4] That exceptional moment – broadly defined at the international level by embedded liberalism, at the national level by social democratic consensus, and at the economic level by Fordism – has been falling apart since the 1970s.

What characterised the postwar situation of the high-income economies? For our purposes, two elements are crucial (though not exhaustive): the business model and the nature of employment. After the devastation of the Second World War, American manufacturing was in a globally dominant position. It was marked by large manufacturing plants built along Fordist lines, with the automobile industry functioning as the paradigm. These factories were oriented towards mass production, top-down managerial control, and a 'just in case' approach that demanded extra workers and extra inventories in case of surges in demand. The labour process was organised along Taylorist principles, which sought to break tasks down into smaller deskilled pieces and to reorganise them in the most efficient way; and workers were gathered together in large numbers in single factories. This gave rise to the mass worker, capable of developing a collective identity on the basis of fellow workers' sharing in the same conditions. Workers in this period were represented by trade unions that reached a balance with capital and repressed more radical initiatives.[5] Collective bargaining ensured that wages grew at a healthy pace, and workers were increasingly bundled into manufacturing industries with relatively permanent jobs, high wages, and guaranteed pensions. Meanwhile the welfare state redistributed money to those left outside the labour market.

As its nearest competitors were devastated by the war, American manufacturing profited and was the powerhouse of the postwar era.[6] Yet Japan and Germany had their own comparative advantages – notably relatively low labour costs, skilled labour forces, advantageous exchange rates, and, in Japan's case, a highly supportive institutional structure between government, banks, and key firms. Furthermore, the American Marshall Plan laid the groundwork for expanding export markets and for rising investment levels across these countries. Between the 1950s and the 1960s Japanese and German manufacturing grew rapidly in terms of output and productivity. Most importantly, as the world market developed and global demand grew, Japanese and German firms began to cut into the share of American firms. Suddenly there were multiple major manufacturers that produced for the world market. The consequence was that global manufacturing reached a point of overcapacity and overproduction that put downward pressure on the prices of manufactured goods. By the mid-1960s, American manufacturing was being undercut in terms of prices by its Japanese and German competitors, which led to a crisis of profitability for domestic firms. The high, fixed costs of the United States were simply no longer able to beat the prices of its competitors. Through a series of exchange rate adaptations, this crisis of profitability was eventually transmitted to Japan and Germany, and the global crisis of the 1970s was underway.

In the face of declining profitability, manufacturers made efforts to revive their businesses. In the first place, firms turned to their successful competitors and began to model themselves after them. The American Fordist model was to be replaced by the Japanese Toyotist model.[7] In terms of the labour process, production was to be streamlined. A sort of hyper-Taylorism aimed to break the process down into its smallest components and to ensure that as few impediments and downtime entered into the sequence. The entire process was reorganised to be as lean as possible. Companies were increasingly told by shareholders and management consultants to cut back to their core competencies, any excess workers being laid off and inventories kept to a minimum. This was mandated and enabled by the rise of increasingly sophisticated supply chain software, as manufacturers would demand and expect supplies to arrive as needed. And there was a move away from the mass production of homogeneous goods and towards increasingly customised goods that responded to consumer demand. Yet these efforts met with counter-attempts by Japanese and German competitors to increase their own profitability, along with the introduction of new competitors (Korea, Taiwan, Singapore, and eventually China). The result was continued international competition, overcapacity, and downward pressures on prices.

The second major attempt to revive profitability was through an attack on the power of labour. Unions across the western world faced an all-out assault and were eventually broken. Trade unions faced new legal hurdles, the deregulation of various industries, and a subsequent decline in membership. Businesses took advantage of this to reduce wages and increasingly to outsource jobs. Early outsourcing involved jobs with goods that could be shipped (e.g. small consumer goods), while non-tradable services (e.g. administration) and non-tradable goods (e.g. houses) remained. Yet in the 1990s information and communications technologies enabled a number of those services to be offshored, and the relevant distinction came to be the one between services that required face-to-face encounters (e.g. haircuts, care work) and impersonal services that did not (e.g. data entry, customer service, radiologists, etc.).[8] The former were contracted out domestically where possible, while the latter were under increasing pressure from global labour markets. Hospitality provides one illuminating example of this general trend: the percentage of franchised hotels in the United States raised from a marginal figure in the 1960s to over 76 per cent by 2006. Alongside this, there was a move towards contracting all other work associated with hospitality: cleaning, management, maintenance, and janitorial services.[9]

The drivers behind this shift were to reduce benefits and liability costs, in an effort to maintain profitability levels. These changes inaugurated the secular trends we have seen since, with employment being increasingly flexible, low wage, and subject to pressures from management.

The Dot-com Boom and Bust

The 1970s therefore set the stage for the lengthy slump in manufacturing profitability that has since been the baseline of advanced economies. A period of healthy manufacturing growth in the United States began when the dollar was devalued in the Plaza Accord (1985); but manufacturing slumped again when the yen and the mark were devalued over fears of Japanese collapse.[10] And, while economic growth recovered from its 1970s lows, nevertheless the G7 countries have all seen both economic and productivity growth trend downwards.[11] The one notable exception was the dot-com boom in the 1990s and its associated frenzy of interest in the possibilities of the internet. In fact the 1990s' boom is redolent of much of today's fascination with the sharing economy, the internet of things, and other tech-enabled businesses. It will remain to the next chapter to show us whether the fate of these recent developments will follow the same downward path as well. For our present purposes, the most significant aspects of the 1990s' boom and bust are the installation of an infrastructural basis for the digital economy and the turn to an ultra-accommodative monetary policy in response to economic problems.

The boom in the 1990s amounted effectively to the fateful commercialisation of what had been, until that point, a largely non-commercial internet. It was an era driven by financial speculation, which was in turn fostered by large amounts of venture capital (VC) and expressed in high levels of stock valuation. As US manufacturing began to stall after the reversal of the Plaza Accord, the telecommunications sector became the favoured outlet of financial capital in the late 1990s. It was a vast new sector, and the imperative for profit latched onto the possibilities afforded by getting people and businesses online. When this sector was at its height, nearly 1 per cent of US gross domestic product (GDP) consisted of VC invested in tech companies; and the average size of VC deals quadrupled between 1996 and

2000.[12] All told, more than 50,000 companies were formed to commercialise the internet and more than $256 billion was provided to them.[13] Investors chased hopes for future profitability and companies adopted a 'growth before profits' model. While many of these businesses lacked a revenue source and, even more, lacked any profits, the hope was that through rapid growth they would be able to grab market share and eventually dominate what was assumed to be a major new industry. In what would come to characterise the internet-based sector to this day, it appeared a requirement that companies aim for monopolistic dominance. In the cut-throat early stages investors enthusiastically joined, in hopes of picking the eventual winner. Many companies did not have to rely on VC either, as the equity markets swooned over tech stocks. Initially driven by declining borrowing costs and rising corporate profits,[14] the stock market boom came unmoored from the real economy when it latched onto the 'new economy' promised by internet-based companies. During its peak period between 1997 and 2000, technology stocks rose 300 per cent and took on a market capitalisation of $5 trillion.[15]

This excitement about the new industry

translated into a massive injection of capital into the fixed assets of the internet. While investment in computers and information technology had been going on for decades, the level of investment in the period between 1995 and 2000 remains unprecedented to this day. In 1980 the level of annual investment in computers and peripheral equipment was \$50.1 billion; by 1990 it had reached \$154.6 billion; and at the height of the bubble, in 2000, it reached an unsurpassed peak of \$412.8 billion.[16] This was a global shift as well: in the low-income economies, telecommunications was the largest sector for foreign direct investment in the 1990s – with over \$331 billion invested in it.[17] Companies began spending extraordinary amounts to modernise their computing infrastructure and, in conjunction with a series of regulatory changes introduced by the US government,[18] this laid the basis for the mainstreaming of the internet in the early years of the new millennium. Concretely, this investment meant that millions of miles of fibre-optic and submarine cables were laid out, major advances in software and network design were established, and large investments in databases and servers were made. This process also accelerated the outsourcing tendency initiated in the 1970s, when coordination costs were drastically cut as global communication and supply chains became easier to build and manage.[19] Companies pushed more and more of their components outwards and Nike became an emblem of the lean firm: branding and design were managed in the high-income economies, while manufacturing and assembly were outsourced to sweatshops in the low-income economies. In all of these ways, the 1990s tech boom was a bubble that laid the groundwork for the digital economy to come.

In 1998, as the East Asian crisis gathered pace, the US boom began to stumble as well. The bust was staved off through a series of rapid interest rate reductions made by the US Federal Reserve; and these reductions marked the beginning of a lengthy period of ultra-easy monetary policy. Implicitly the goal was to let equity markets continue to rise despite their 'irrational exuberance',[20] in an effort to increase the nominal wealth of companies and households and hence their propensity to invest and consume. In a world where the US government was trying to reduce its deficits, fiscal stimulus was out of the question. This 'asset-price Keynesianism' offered an alternative way to get the economy growing in the absence of deficit spending and competitive manufacturing.[21] It was a signal shift in the US economy: without a revival of US manufacturing, profitability was necessarily sought in other sectors. And it worked for a time, as it facilitated further investment in new dot-com companies and kept the asset bubble running until 2000, when the National Association of Securities Dealers Automated Quotations (NASDAQ) stock market peaked. Reliance on an accommodative monetary policy continued after the 2001 crash as well,[22] including through lowered interest rates and through a new liquidity provision in the wake of the 9/11 attacks. One of the effects of these central bank interventions was to lower mortgage rates, thereby fostering conditions for a housing bubble. Lowered interest rates also lowered the return on financial investments and compelled a search for new investments – a search that eventually landed on the high returns available from subprime mortgages and set the stage for the next crisis. Loose monetary policy is one of the key consequences of the 1990s bust, and one that continues on to this day.

The Crisis of 2008

In 2006 US housing prices reached a turning point, and their decline began to weigh on the rest of the economy. Household wealth decreased in tandem, leading to lowered consumption and eventually to a series of mortgage non-payments. As the financial system had become increasingly tied to the mortgage market, it was inevitable that the decline in housing prices would wreak havoc on the financial sector. Strains began to emerge in 2007, when two hedge funds collapsed after being heavily involved in mortgage-backed securities. The entire structure buckled in September 2008, when Lehman Brothers collapsed and a full-blown crisis burst asunder.

The immediate response was quick and massive. The US Federal Reserve moved to bail out banks to the tune of $700 billion, provided liquidity assistance, extended the scope of deposit insurance, and even took partial ownership of key banks. Through massive bailouts, support for faltering companies, emergency tax cuts, and a series of automatic stabilisers, governments undertook the burden of increasing their deficits in order to ward off the worst of the crisis. As a result, the high levels of private debt before the crisis were transformed into high levels of public debt after the crisis. Simultaneously, central banks stepped in to try and prevent a breakdown of the global financial order. The United States initiated a number of liquidity actions designed to make sure that the pipelines of credit kept running. Emergency lending was made to banks, and currency swap agreements were drawn up with 14 different countries in order to ensure that they had access to the dollars they needed. The most important action, however, was that key interest rates across the world dropped precipitously: the US federal funds target rate went from 5.25 per cent in August 2007 to a 0–0.25 per cent target by December 2008. Likewise, the Bank of England dropped its primary interest rate from 5.0 per cent in October 2008 to 0.5 per cent by March 2009. October 2008 saw the crisis intensify, which led to an internationally coordinated interest rate cut by six major central banks. By 2016 monetary policymakers had dropped interest rates 637 times.[23] This has continued through the postcrisis period and has established a low interest rate environment for the global economy – a key enabling condition for parts of today's digital economy to arise.

But, when the immediate threat of collapse was gone, governments were suddenly left with a massive bill. After decades of increasing government deficits, the 2008 crisis pushed a number of governments into a seemingly more precarious position. The United States saw its deficit rise from $160 million to $1,412 million over 2007–9. In part from fears of the effects of high government debt, in part as a means to build up the fiscal resources for any future crisis, and in part as a class project intended to continue the privatisation and reduction of the state, austerity became the watchword in advanced capitalist nations. Governments were to eliminate their deficits and reduce their debts. While other countries have faced deeper cuts to government spending, the United States has not escaped the dominance of austerity ideology. At the end of 2012 a series of tax raises and spending cuts were brought in, while at the same time tax cuts that had been implemented in response to the crisis were allowed to expire. Since 2011 the deficit has been reduced every year. Perhaps the biggest influence of austerity ideas on America, however, was the political impossibility of getting any major new fiscal stimulus. The United States has a significantly decaying infrastructure, but even here the argument for government spending falls on deaf ears. This has reached its peak in the political posturing that occurs increasingly frequently over the US debt ceiling. This congressionally approved ceiling sets a limit on how much debt the US Treasury can issue and has become a major point of contention between those who think that the US debt is too high and those who think that spending is necessary.

Since fiscal stimulus is politically unpalatable, governments have been left with only one mechanism for reviving their sluggish economies: monetary policy. The result has been a series of extraordinary and unprecedented central bank interventions. We have already noted a continuation of low interest rate policies. But, stuck at the zero lower bound, policymakers have been forced to turn toward more unconventional monetary instruments.[24] The most important of these has been 'quantitative easing': the creation of money by the central bank, which then uses that money to purchase various assets (e.g. government bonds, corporate bonds, mortgages) from the banks. The United States led the way in using quantitative easing in November 2008, while the United Kingdom followed suit in March 2009. The European Central Bank (ECB), due to its unique situation as a central bank of numerous countries, was slower to act, although it eventually began purchasing government bonds in January 2015. By the beginning of 2016, central banks across the world had purchased more than $12.3 trillion worth of assets.[25] The primary argument for using quantitative easing is that it should lower the yields of other assets. If traditional monetary policy operates primarily by altering the short-term interest rate, quantitative easing seeks to affect the interest rates of longer term and alternative assets. The key idea here is a 'portfolio balance channel'. Given that assets are not perfect substitutes for one another (they have different values, different risks, different returns), taking away or restricting supply of one asset should have an effect on demand for other assets. In particular, reducing the supply of government bonds should increase the demand for other financial assets. It should both lower the yield of bonds (e.g. corporate debt), thereby easing credit, and raise the asset prices of stocks (e.g. corporate equities) and subsequently create a wealth effect to spur spending. While the evidence is still preliminary, it does seem that quantitative easing has had an effect in this way: corporate yields have declined and stock markets have surged upwards.[26] It may have had an effect on the non-financial sectors of the economy as well, by making much of the economic recovery dependent on $4.7 trillion of new corporate debt since 2007.[27] Most important for our purpose is the fact that the generalised low interest rate environment built by central banks has reduced the rate of return on a wide range of financial assets. The result is that investors seeking higher yields have had to turn to increasingly risky assets – by investing in unprofitable and unproven tech companies, for instance.

In addition to a loose monetary policy, there has been a significant growth in corporate cash hoarding and tax havens in recent years. In the United States, as of January 2016, $1.9 trillion is being held by companies in cash and cash-like investments – that is, in low-interest, liquid securities.[28] This is part of a long-term and global trend towards higher levels of corporate savings;[29] but the rise in cash hoarding has accelerated with

Table 1.1   Reserves, onshore and offshore

	Reserves (billions of USD)	Amount held offshore (billions of USD)	Amount held offshore (per cent)
Apple	215.7	200.1	92.8
Microsoft	102.6	96.3	93.9
Google	73.1	42.9	58.7
Cisco	60.4	56.5	93.5
Oracle	50.8	46.8	92.1
Amazon	49.6	18.3	36.9
Facebook	15.8	1.8	11.4
TOTAL	568.0	462.7	81.5

Source: 10-Q or 10-K Securities and Exchange Commission (SEC) filings from March 2016

the surge in corporate profits after the crisis. Moreover, with a few exceptions such as General Motors, it is a phenomenon dominated by tech companies. Since these companies only need to move intellectual property (rather than entire factories) to different tax jurisdictions, tax evasion is particularly easy for them. Table 1.1 outlines the amount of reserves[30] held by some of the major tech companies, and also the amount held offshore by foreign subsidiaries.

These figures are enormous: Google's total is enough to purchase Uber or Goldman Sachs, while Apple's reserves are enough to buy

Samsung, Pfizer, or Shell. To properly understand these figures, however, some caveats are in order. In the first place, they do not take into account the respective companies' liabilities and debt. However, with historically low corporate yields, many companies find it cheaper to take on new debt instead of repatriating these offshore funds and paying corporate tax on them. In their SEC filings tax avoidance is explicitly given as a reason for holding such high levels of offshore reserves. The use of corporate debt by these companies therefore needs to be set in the context of a tax avoidance strategy. This is also part of a broader trend towards the growing use of tax havens. In the wake of the crisis, offshore wealth grew by 25 per cent between 2008 and 2014,[31] which resulted in an estimated $7.6 trillion of household financial wealth being held in tax havens.[32] The point of all this is twofold. At one end, tax evasion and cash hoarding have left US companies – particularly tech companies – with a vast amount of money to invest. This glut of corporate savings has – both directly and indirectly – combined with a loose monetary policy to strengthen the pursuit of riskier investments for the sake of a decent return. At the other end, tax evasion is, by definition, a drain on government revenues and therefore has exacerbated austerity. The vast amount of tax money that goes missing in tax havens must be made up elsewhere. The result is further limitations on fiscal stimulus and a greater need for unorthodox monetary policies. Tax evasion, austerity, and extraordinary monetary policies are all mutually reinforcing.

To define the present conjuncture, we must add one further element: the employment situation. With the collapse of communism, there has been a long-term trend towards both greater proletarianisation and greater numbers of surplus populations.[33] Much of the world today receives a market-mediated income through precarious and informal work. This reserve army was significantly expanded after the 2008 crisis. The initial shock of the crisis meant that unemployment jumped drastically across the board. In the United States it doubled, going from 5.0 per cent before the crisis to 10.0 per cent at its height. Among the unemployed, long-term unemployment escalated from 17.4 per cent to 45.5 per cent: not only did many people lose their jobs, they did so for long periods of time. Even today, long-term unemployment remains at levels higher than anything seen before the crisis. The effect of all this has been pressure on the remaining employed population – lower weekly earnings, fewer household savings, and increased household debt. In the United States personal savings have been declining from above 10.0 per cent in the 1970s to around 5.0 per cent after the crisis.[34] In the United Kingdom household savings have decreased to 3.8 per cent – a 50-year low and a secular trend since the 1990s.[35] In this context, many have been forced to take whatever job is available.

Conclusion

The conjuncture today is therefore a product of long-term trends and cyclical movements. We continue to live in a capitalist society where competition and profit seeking provide the general parameters of our world. But the 1970s created a major shift within these general conditions, away from secure employment and unwieldy industrial behemoths and towards flexible labour and lean business models. During the 1990s a technological revolution was laid out when finance drove a bubble in the new internet industry that led to massive investment in the built environment. This phenomenon also heralded a turn towards a new model of growth: America was definitively giving up on its manufacturing base and turning towards asset-price Keynesianism as the best viable option. This new model of growth led to the housing bubble of the early twenty-first century and has driven the response to the 2008 crisis. Plagued by global concerns over public debt, governments have turned to monetary policy in order to ease economic conditions. This, combined with increases in corporate savings and with the expansion of tax havens, has let loose a vast glut of cash, which has been seeking out decent rates of investment in a low-interest rate world. Finally, workers have suffered immensely in the wake of the crisis and have been highly vulnerable to exploitative working conditions as a result of their need to earn an income. All this sets the scene for today's economy.

2

Platform Capitalism

Capitalism, when a crisis hits, tends to be restructured. New technologies, new organisational forms, new modes of exploitation, new types of jobs, and new markets all emerge to create a new way of accumulating capital. As we saw with the crisis of overcapacity in the 1970s, manufacturing attempted to recover by attacking labour and by turning towards increasingly lean business models. In the wake of the 1990s bust, internet-based companies shifted to business models that monetised the free resources available to them. While the dot-com bust placed a pall over investor enthusiasm for internet-based firms, the subsequent decade saw technology firms significantly progressing in terms of the amount of power and capital at their disposal. Since the 2008 crisis, has there been a similar shift? The dominant narrative in the advanced capitalist countries *has* been one of change. In particular, there has been a renewed focus on the rise of technology: automation, the sharing economy, endless stories about the 'Uber for X', and, since around 2010, proclamations about the internet of things. These changes have received labels such as 'paradigm shift' from McKinsey[1] and 'fourth industrial revolution' from the executive chairman of the World Economic Forum and, in more ridiculous formulations, have been compared in importance to the Renaissance and the Enlightenment.[2] We have witnessed a massive proliferation of new terms: the gig economy, the sharing economy, the on-demand economy, the next industrial revolution, the surveillance economy, the app economy, the attention economy, and so on. The task of this chapter is to examine these changes.

Numerous theorists have argued that these changes mean we live in a cognitive, or informational, or immaterial, or knowledge economy. But what does this mean? Here we can find a number of interconnected but distinct claims. In

Italian autonomism, this would be a claim about the 'general intellect', where *collective cooperation and knowledge become a source of value*.[3] Such an argument also entails that the *labour process is increasingly immaterial*, oriented towards the use and manipulation of symbols and affects. Likewise, the traditional industrial working class is increasingly replaced by *knowledge workers* or the 'cognitariat'. Simultaneously, the generalised deindustrialisation of the high-income economies means that *the product of work becomes immaterial*: cultural content, knowledge, affects, and services. This includes media content like YouTube and blogs, as well as broader contributions in the form of creating websites, participating in online forums, and producing software.[4] A related claim is that *material commodities contain an increasing amount of knowledge*, which is embodied in them. The production process of even the most basic agricultural commodities, for instance, is reliant upon a vast array of scientific and technical knowledges. On the other side of the class relation, some argue that the economy today is dominated by a new class, which does not own the means of production but rather has *ownership over information*.[5] There is some truth in this, but

38

the argument goes awry when it situates this class outside of capitalism. Given that the imperatives of capitalism hold for these companies as much as for any other, the companies remain capitalist. Yet there is something new here, and it is worth trying to discern exactly what it is.

A key argument of this chapter is that in the twenty-first century advanced capitalism came to be centred upon extracting and using a particular kind of raw material: data. But it is important to be clear about what data are. In the first place, we will distinguish *data* (information that something happened) from *knowledge* (information about why something happened). Data may involve knowledge, but this is not a necessary condition. Data also entail recording, and therefore a material medium of some kind. As a recorded entity, any datum requires sensors to capture it and massive storage systems to maintain it. Data are not immaterial, as any glance at the energy consumption of data centres will quickly prove (and the internet as a whole is responsible for about 9.2 per cent of the world's electricity consumption).[6] We should also be wary of thinking that data collection and analysis are frictionless or automated processes. Most data must be cleaned and organised into standardised formats in order to be usable. Likewise, generating the proper algorithms can involve the manual entry of learning sets into a system. Altogether, this means that the collection of data today is dependent on a vast infrastructure to sense, record, and analyse.[7] What is recorded? Simply put, we should consider *data* to be the raw material that must be extracted, and the *activities* of users to be the natural source of this raw material.[8] Just like oil, data are a material to be extracted, refined, and used in a variety of ways. The more data one has, the more uses one can make of them.

Data were a resource that had been available for some time and used to lesser degrees in previous business models (particularly in coordinating the global logistics of lean production). In the twenty-first century, however, the technology needed for turning simple activities into recorded data became increasingly cheap; and the move to digital-based communications made recording exceedingly simple. Massive new expanses of potential data were opened up, and new industries arose to extract these data and to use them so as to optimise production processes, give insight into consumer preferences, control workers, provide the foundation for new products and services (e.g. Google Maps, self-driving cars, Siri), and sell to advertisers. All of this had historical precedents in earlier periods of capitalism, but what was novel with the shift in technology was the sheer amount of data that could now be used. From representing a peripheral aspect of businesses, data increasingly became a central resource. In the early years of the century it was hardly clear, however, that data would become the raw material to jumpstart a major shift in capitalism.[9] The incipient efforts by Google simply used data to draw advertising revenues away from traditional media outlets like newspapers and television. Google was performing a valuable service in organising the internet, but this was hardly a revolutionary change at an economic level. However, as the internet expanded and firms became dependent on digital communications for all aspects of their business, data became increasingly relevant. As I will attempt to show in this chapter, data have come to serve a number of key capitalist functions: they educate and give competitive advantage to algorithms; they enable the coordination and outsourcing of workers; they allow for the optimisation and flexibility of productive processes; they make possible the transformation of low-margin goods into high-margin services; and data analysis is itself generative of data, in a virtuous cycle. Given the significant advantages of recording and using data and the competitive pressures of capitalism, it was perhaps inevitable that this raw material would come to represent a vast new resource to be extracted from.

The problem for capitalist firms that continues to the present day is that old business models were not particularly well designed to extract and use data. Their method of operating was to produce a good in a factory where most of the information was lost, then to sell it, and never to learn anything about the customer or how the product was being used. While the global logistics network of lean production was an improvement in this respect, with few exceptions it remained a lossy model as well. A different business model was necessary if capitalist firms were to take full advantage of dwindling recording costs. This chapter argues that the new business model that eventually emerged is a powerful new type of firm: the platform.[10] Often arising out of internal needs to handle data, platforms became an efficient way to monopolise, extract, analyse, and use the increasingly large amounts of data that were being recorded. Now this model has come to expand across the economy, as numerous companies incorporate platforms: powerful technology companies (Google, Facebook, and Amazon), dynamic start-ups (Uber, Airbnb), industrial leaders (GE, Siemens), and agricultural powerhouses (John Deere, Monsanto), to name just a few.

What are platforms?[11] At the most general level, platforms are digital infrastructures that enable two or more groups to interact.[12] They therefore position themselves as intermediaries that bring together different users: customers, advertisers, service providers, producers, suppliers, and even physical objects.[13] More often than not, these platforms also come with a series of tools that enable their users to build their own products, services, and marketplaces.[14] Microsoft's Windows operating system enables software developers to create applications for it and sell them to consumers; Apple's App Store and its associated ecosystem (XCode and the iOS SDK) enable developers to build and sell new apps to users; Google's search engine provides a platform for advertisers and content providers to target people searching for information; and Uber's taxi app enables drivers and passengers to exchange rides for cash. Rather than having to build a marketplace from the ground up, a platform provides the basic infrastructure to mediate between different groups. This is the key to its advantage over traditional business models when it comes to data, since a platform positions itself (1) between users, and (2) as the ground upon which their activities occur, which thus gives it privileged access to record them. Google, as the platform for searching, draws on vast amounts of search activity (which express the fluctuating desires of individuals). Uber, as the platform for taxis, draws on traffic data and the activities of drivers and riders. Facebook, as the platform for social networking, brings in a variety of intimate social interactions that can then be recorded. And, as more and more industries move their interactions online (e.g. Uber shifting the taxi industry into a digital form), more and more businesses will be subject to platform development. Platforms are, as a result, far more than internet companies or tech companies, since they can operate anywhere, wherever digital interaction takes place.

The second essential characteristic is that digital platforms produce and are reliant on 'network effects': the more numerous the users who use a platform, the more valuable that platform becomes for everyone else. Facebook, for example, has become the default social networking platform simply by virtue of the sheer number of people on it. If you want to join a platform for socialising, you join the platform where most of your friends and family already are. Likewise, the more numerous the users who search on Google, the better their search algorithms become, and the more useful Google becomes to users. But this generates a cycle whereby more users beget more users, which leads to platforms having a natural tendency towards monopolisation. It also lends platforms a dynamic of ever-increasing access to more activities, and therefore to more data. Moreover, the ability to rapidly scale many platform businesses by relying on pre-existing infrastructure and cheap marginal costs means that there are few natural limits to growth. One reason for Uber's rapid growth, for instance, is that it does not need to build new factories – it just needs to rent more servers. Combined with network effects, this means that platforms can grow very big very quickly.

The importance of network effects means that platforms must deploy a range of tactics to ensure that more and more users come on board. For example – and this is the third characteristic – platforms often use cross-subsidisation: one arm of the firm reduces the price of a service or good (even providing it for free), but another arm raises prices in order to make up for these losses. The price structure of the platform matters significantly for how many users become involved and how often they use the platform.[15] Google, for instance, provides service likes email for free in order to get users on board, but raises money through its advertising arm. Since platforms have to attract a number of different groups, part of their business is fine-tuning the balance between what is paid, what is not paid, what is subsidised, and what is not subsidised. This is a far cry from the lean model, which aimed to reduce a company down to its core competencies and sell off any unprofitable ventures.[16]

Finally, platforms are also designed in a way that makes them attractive to its varied users. While often presenting themselves as empty spaces for others to interact on, they in fact embody a politics. The rules of product and service development, as well as marketplace interactions, are set by the platform owner. Uber, despite presenting itself as an empty vessel for market forces, shapes the appearance of a market. It predicts where the demand for drivers will be and raises surge prices in advance of actual demand, while also creating phantom cabs to give an illusion of greater supply.[17] In their position as an intermediary, platforms gain not only access to more data but also control and governance over the rules of the game. The core architecture of fixed rules, however, is also generative, enabling others to build upon them in unexpected ways. The core architecture of Facebook, for instance, has allowed developers to produce apps, companies to create pages, and users to share information in a way that brings in even more users. The same holds for Apple's App Store, which enabled the production of numerous useful apps that tied users and software developers increasingly into its ecosystem. The challenge of maintaining platforms is, in part, to revise the cross-subsidisation links and the rules of the platform in order to sustain user interest. While network effects strongly support existing platform leaders, these positions are not unassailable. Platforms, in sum, are a new type of firm; they are characterised by providing the infrastructure to intermediate between different user groups, by displaying monopoly tendencies driven by network effects, by employing cross-subsidisation to draw in different user groups, and by having a designed core architecture that governs the interaction possibilities. Platform ownership, in turn, is essentially ownership of software (the 2 billion lines of code for Google, or the 20 million lines of code for Facebook)[18] and hardware (servers, data centres, smart-phones, etc.), built upon open-source material (e.g. Hadoop's data management system is used by Facebook).[19] All these characteristics make platforms key business models for extracting and controlling data. By providing a digital space for others to interact in, platforms position them-selves so as to extract data from natural processes (weather conditions, crop cycles, etc.), from pro-duction processes (assembly lines, continuous flow manufacturing, etc.), and from other busi-nesses and users (web tracking, usage data, etc.). They are an extractive apparatus for data.

The remainder of this chapter will give an

overview of the emerging platform landscape by way of presenting five different types of platforms. In each of these areas, the important element is that the capitalist class owns the platform, not necessarily that it produces a physical product. The first type is that of *advertising platforms* (e.g. Google, Facebook), which extract information on users, undertake a labour of analysis, and then use the products of that process to sell ad space. The second type is that of *cloud platforms* (e.g. AWS, Salesforce), which own the hardware and software of digital-dependent businesses and are renting them out as needed. The third type is that of *industrial platforms* (e.g. GE, Siemens), which build the hardware and software necessary to transform traditional manufacturing into internet-connected processes that lower the costs of production and transform goods into services. The fourth type is that of *product platforms* (e.g. Rolls Royce, Spotify), which generate revenue by using other platforms to transform a traditional good into a service and by collecting rent or subscription fees on them. Finally, the fifth type is that of *lean platforms* (e.g. Uber, Airbnb), which attempt to reduce their ownership of assets to a minimum and to profit by reducing costs as much as possible. These analytical divisions can, and often do, run together within any one firm. Amazon, for example, is often seen as an e-commerce company, yet it rapidly broadened out into a logistics company. Today it is spreading into the on-demand market with a Home Services program in partnership with TaskRabbit, while the infamous Mechanical Turk (AMT) was in many ways a pioneer for the gig economy and, perhaps most importantly, is developing Amazon Web Services as a cloud-based service. Amazon therefore spans nearly all of the above categories.

Advertising Platforms

The elders of this new enterprise form, advertising platforms are the initial attempts at building a model adequate to the digital age. As we will see, they have directly and indirectly fostered the emergence of the most recent technological trends – from the sharing economy to the industrial internet. They emerged out of the easy credit-fuelled dot-com bust, whose effect was twofold. One aspect of it was that many competitors collapsed, leaving the various areas of the tech industry increasingly under the control of the remaining enterprises. The sudden unwillingness of venture capital (VC) to finance new entries meant that entry into the competitive landscape remained closed as well. The monopoly tendencies of the early tech boom were solidified here, as a new range of dominant companies emerged from the ashes and have continued to dominate ever since. The other important consequence of the bust was that the drying up of VC and equity financing placed new pressure on internet-based companies to generate revenues. In the midst of the boom there was no clearly dominant way to raise a sustainable revenue stream – companies were relatively equally divided among different proposals.[20] However, the centrality of marketing to finance capital's 'growth before profits' strategy meant that dot-com firms had already built the basis for a business model oriented towards advertising and attracting users. As a percentage of revenues, these firms spent 3–4 times more than other sectors on advertising, and they were the pioneers in purchasing online advertising as well.[21] When the bubble burst, it was perhaps inevitable that these companies would turn towards advertising as their major revenue source. In this endeavour, Google and Facebook have come to represent the leading edges of this process.

Created in 1997, Google was an early recipient of venture funding in 1998 and received a major $25 million funding round in 1999. At this point Google had been collecting user data from searches and using these data to improve searches.[22] This was an example of the classic use of data within capitalism: it was meant to improve one's services for customers and users. But there was no value leftover from which Google could generate revenue. In the wake of the dot-com bust, Google increasingly needed a way to generate revenues, yet a fee-based service risked alienating the users who were the basis of its success. Eventually it began to use the search data, along with cookies and other bits of information, to sell targeted ad space to advertisers through an increasingly automated auction system.[23] When the National Association of Securities Dealers Automated Quotations (NASDAQ) market peaked in March 2000, Google unveiled AdWords in October 2000 and began its transformation into a revenue-generating company. The extracted data moved from being a way to improve services to becoming a way to collect advertising revenues.

Today Google and Facebook remain almost entirely dependent on them: in the first quarter of 2016, 89.0 per cent of Google's and 96.6 per cent of Facebook's revenues came from advertisers.

This was part and parcel of the broader shift, in the early years of the new millennium, to Web 2.0, which was premised more on user-generated content than on digital storefronts and on multimedia interfaces rather than on static text. In the press, this shift came packaged with a rhetoric of democratising communication in which anyone would be able to create and share content online. No longer would newspapers and other mass media outlets have a monopoly over what was voiced in society. For critical theorists of the web, this rhetoric obscured a shift to business models premised upon the exploitation of 'free labour'.[24] From this perspective, the story of how Google and Facebook generate profit has been a simple one: users are unwaged labourers who produce goods (data and content) that are then taken and sold by the companies to advertisers and other interested parties. There are a number of problems with this account, however. A first issue with the free labour argument is that it often slides into grand metaphysical claims. *All* social inter-action becomes free labour for capitalism, and we begin to worry that there is no outside to capitalism. Work becomes inseparable from non-work and precise categories become blunt banalities. It is important, however, to draw distinctions between interactions done on plat-forms and interactions done elsewhere, as well as between interactions done on profit-oriented platforms and interactions done on other plat-forms.[25] Not all – and not even most – of our social interactions are co-opted into a system of profit generation. In fact one of the reasons why companies must compete to build platforms is that most of our social interactions do *not* enter into a valorisation process. If all of our actions were already captured within capitalist valorisa-tion, it is hard to see why there would be a need to build the extractive apparatus of platforms. More broadly, 'free labour' is only a portion of the multitude of data sources that a company like Google relies upon: economic transactions, information collected by sensors in the inter-net of things, corporate and government data (such as credit records and financial records), and public and private surveillance (such as the cars used to build up Google Maps).[26]

Yet even limiting our attention to user-created data, it is right to call this activity *labour*? Within a Marxist framework, labour has a very particular meaning: it is an activity that generates a surplus value within a context of markets for labour and a production process oriented towards exchange. The debate over whether or not online social interaction is part of capitalist production is not just a tedious scholarly debate over definitions. The relevance of whether this interaction is free labour or not has to do with consequences. If it is capitalist, then it will be pressured by all the standard capitalist imperatives: to rationalise the production processes, to lower costs, to increase productivity, and so on. If it is not, then those demands will not be imposed. In examining the activities of users online, it is hard to make the case that what they do is labour, properly speaking. Beyond the intuitive hesitation to think that messaging friends is labour, any idea of socially necessary labour time – the implicit standard against which production processes are set – is lacking. This means there are no competitive pressures for getting users to *do* more, even if there are pressures to get them to do more online. More broadly, if our online interactions are free labour, then these companies must be a significant boon to capitalism overall – a whole new landscape of exploited labour has been opened up. On the other hand, if this is not free labour, then these firms are parasitical on other value-producing industries and global capitalism is in a more dire state. A quick glance at the stagnating global economy suggests that the latter is more likely.

Rather than exploiting free labour, the position taken here is that advertising platforms appropriate data as a raw material. The activities of users and institutions, if they are recorded and transformed into data, become a raw material that can be refined and used in a variety of ways by platforms. With advertising platforms in particular, revenue is generated through the extraction of data from users' activities online, from the analysis of those data, and from the auctioning of ad space to advertisers. This involves achieving two processes. First, advertising platforms need to monitor and record online activities. The more users interact with a site, the more information can be collected and used. Equally, as users wander around the internet, they are tracked via cookies and other means, and these data become ever more extensive and valuable to advertisers. There is a convergence of surveillance and profit making in the digital economy, which leads some to speak of 'surveillance capitalism'.[27] Key to revenues, however, is not just the collection of data, but also the analysis of data. Advertisers are interested less in unorganised data and more in data that give them insights or match them to likely consumers. These are data that have been *worked on*.[28] They have had some process applied to them, whether through the skilled labour of a data scientist or the automated labour of a machine-learning algorithm. What is sold to advertisers is therefore not the data themselves (advertisers do not receive personalised data), but rather the promise that Google's software will adeptly match an advertiser with the correct users when needed.

While the data extraction model has been prominent in the online world, it has also migrated into the offline world. Tesco, one of the world's largest retailers, owns Dunnhumby, a UK-based 'consumer insights' business valued at around $2 billion. (The US arm of the company was recently sold to Kroger, one of America's largest employers.) The company is premised upon tracking consumers both online and offline and using that information to sell to clients such as Coca-Cola, Macy's, and Office Depot. It has attempted to build a monopolistic platform for itself as well, through a loyalty card that channels customers into Tesco stores with the promise of rewards. Simultaneously, more and more diverse information about customers is being tracked (to the point where the company is even suggesting using wearables as a source of customer health data).[29] Non-tech firms are also developing user databases and using data to adapt to customer trends and effectively market goods to consumers. Data extraction is becoming a key method of building a monopolistic platform and of siphoning off revenue from advertisers.

These advertising platforms are currently the most successful of the new platform businesses, with high revenues, significant profits, and a vigorous dynamism. But what have they been doing with their revenues? Investment levels remain low in the United States, United Kingdom, and Germany, so there has been little growth in fixed capital. Instead these companies have tended to do three things with their cash. One was to save it, and high levels of corporate cash have been an odd phenomenon of the post-2008 era. As we saw in Chapter 1, tech companies have taken up a disproportionately large amount of this cash glut. The leaders of tax evasion have also been tech companies: Google, Apple, Facebook, Amazon, and Uber. The second use of this cash was in high levels of mergers and acquisitions – a process that centralises existing capacity rather than building new capacity. Among the big tech companies, Google has made the most acquisitions over the past five years (on average, it purchases a new company every week),[30] while Facebook has some of the biggest acquisitions (e.g. it bought WhatsApp for $22 billion).[31] Google's creation of the Alphabet Holding Company in 2015 is part and parcel of this process; this was an effort designed to enable Google to purchase firms in other industries while giving them a clear delineation from its core business. Thirdly, these companies have funnelled their money into tech start-ups, many of the advertising platforms being large investors in this area. As we will see, they have set the conditions for the latest tech boom. Most importantly, however, they have provided a business model – the platform – that is now being replicated across a variety of industries.

Cloud Platforms

If advertising platforms like Google and Facebook laid the groundwork for extracting and using massive amounts of data, then the emerging cloud platforms are the step that has consolidated the platform as a unique and powerful business model. The story of corporate cloud rental begins with e-commerce in the 1990s. During the late 1990s, e-commerce companies thought they could outsource the material aspects of exchange to others. But this proved to be insufficient, and companies ended up taking on the tasks of building warehouses and logistical networks and hiring large numbers of workers.[32] By 2016 Amazon has invested in vast data centres, robotic warehouse movers, and massive computer systems, had pioneered the use of drones for deliveries, and recently began leasing airplanes for its shipping section.[33] It is also by far the largest employer in the digital economy, employing over 230,000 workers and tens of thousands of seasonal workers, most of whom do low-wage and highly stressful jobs in warehouses. To grow as an e-commerce platform, Amazon has sought to gain as many users as possible through cross-subsidisation. By all accounts, the Amazon Prime delivery service loses money on every order, and the Kindle e-book reader is sold at cost.[34] On traditional metrics for lean businesses, this is unintelligible: unprofitable ventures should be cut off. Yet rapid and cheap delivery is one of the main ways in which Amazon entices users onto its platform in order to make revenues elsewhere.

In the process of building a massive logistical network, Amazon Web Services (AWS) was developed as an internal platform, to handle the increasingly complex logistics of the company. Indeed, a common theme in the genesis of platforms is that they often emerge out of internal company needs. Amazon required ways to get new services up and running quickly, and the answer was to build up the basic infrastructure in a way that enabled new services to use it easily.[35] It was quickly recognised that this could also be rented to other firms. In effect AWS rents out cloud computing services, which include on-demand services for servers, storage and computing power, software development tools

and operating systems, and ready-made applications.[36] The utility of this practice for other
businesses is that they do not need to spend the
time and money to build up their own hardware system, their own software development
kit, or their own applications. They can simply
rent these on an 'as needed' basis. Software, for
instance, is increasingly deployed on a subscription basis; Adobe, Google, and Microsoft have
all started to incorporate this practice. Likewise,
the sophisticated analytical tools that Google has
developed are now beginning to be rented out as
part of its AWS competitor.[37] Other businesses
can now rent the ability to use pattern recogni-
tion algorithms and audio transcription services.
In other words, Google is selling its machine-
learning processes (and this is precisely where
Google sees its advantage over its competitors
in the cloud computing field). Microsoft, meanwhile, has built an artificial intelligence platform
that gives businesses the software development
tools to build their own bots ('intelligence
as a service', in the contemporary lingo). And
International Business Machines (IBM) is
moving to make quantum cloud computing a
reality.[38] Cloud platforms ultimately enable the

outsourcing of much of a company's information technology (IT) department. This process pushes knowledge workers out and often enables the automation of their work as well. Data analysis, storage of customer information, maintenance of a company's servers – all of this can be pushed to the cloud and provides the capitalist rationale for using these platforms.

The logic behind them is akin to how utilities function. Jeff Bezos, Amazon's chief executive officer, compares it to electricity provision: whereas early factories had each its own power generator, eventually electricity generation became centralised and rented out on an 'as needed' basis. Today every area of the economy is increasingly integrated with a digital layer; therefore owning the infrastructure that is necessary to every other industry is an immensely powerful and profitable position to be in. Moreover, the significance of the cloud platform for data extraction is that its rental model enables it to constantly collect data, whereas the older purchasing model involved selling these as goods that were then separated from the company. By moving businesses' activities onto cloud platforms, companies like Amazon gain direct access to whole new datasets (even if some remain occluded to the platform). It is unsurprising, then, that AWS is now estimated to be worth around $70 billion,[39] and major competitors like Microsoft and Google are moving into the field, as well as Chinese competitors like Alibaba. AWS is now the most rapidly growing part of Amazon – and also the most profitable, with about 30 per cent margins and nearly $8 billion in revenue in 2015. In the first quarter of 2016, AWS generated more profit for Amazon than its core retail service.[40] If Google and Facebook built the first data extraction platforms, Amazon built the first major cloud platform in order to rent out an increasingly basic means of production for contemporary businesses. Rather than relying on advertisers' buying data, these cloud platforms are building up the basic infrastructure of the digital economy in a way that can be rented out profitably to others, while they collect data for their own uses.

Industrial Platforms

As data collection, storage, and analysis have become increasingly cheaper, more and more companies have attempted to bring platforms into the field of traditional manufacturing. The most significant of these attempts goes under the rubric of 'the industrial internet of things', or simply 'the industrial internet'. At the most basic level, the industrial internet involves the embedding of sensors and computer chips into the production process and of trackers (e.g. RFID) into the logistics process, all linked together through connections over the internet. In Germany, this process is being heralded as 'Industry 4.0'. The idea is that each component in the production process becomes able to communicate with assembly machines and other components, without the guidance of workers or managers. Data about the position and state of these components are constantly shared with other elements in the production process. In this vision, material goods become inseparable from their informational representations. For its proponents, the industrial internet will optimise the production process: they argue that it is capable of reducing labour costs by 25 per cent, of reducing energy costs by 20 per cent (e.g. data centres would distribute energy where it is needed and when), of reducing maintenance costs by 40 per cent by issuing warnings of wear and tear, of reducing downtime by scheduling it for appropriate times, and of reducing errors and increasing quality.[41] The industrial internet promises, in effect, to make the production process more efficient, primarily by doing what competitive manufacturing has been doing for some time now: reducing costs and downtime. But it also aims to link the production process more closely to the realisation process. Rather than relying on focus groups or surveys, manufacturers are hoping to develop new products and design new features on the basis of usage data drawn from existing products (even by using online methodologies like A/B testing to do so).[42] The industrial internet also enables mass customisation. In one test factory from BASF SE, the largest chemicals producer in the world, the assembly line is capable of individually customising every unit that comes down the line: individual soap bottles can have different fragrances, colours, labels, and soaps, all being automatically produced once a customer places an order.[43] Product lifecycles can be significantly reduced as a result.

As factories begin to implement the components for the industrial internet, one major challenge is establishing a common standard for communication; interoperability between components needs to be ensured, particularly in the case of older machinery. This is where industrial platforms come in, functioning as the basic core framework for linking together sensors and actuators, factories and suppliers, producers and consumers, software and hardware. These are the developing powerhouses of industry, which are building the hardware and software to run the industrial internet across turbines, oil wells, motors, factory floors, trucking fleets, and many more applications. As one report puts it, with the industrial internet 'the big winners will be platform owners'.[44] It is therefore no surprise to see traditional manufacturing powerhouses like General Electric (GE) and Siemens, as well as traditional tech titans like Intel and Microsoft, make a major push to develop industrial internet platforms. Siemens has spent over €4 billion to acquire smart manufacturing capabilities and to build its industrial platform MindSphere,[45] while GE has been working rapidly to develop its own platform, Predix. The field has so far been dominated by these established companies rather than being subject to an influx of new start-ups. And even the industrial internet start-ups are primarily funded by the old guard (four of the top five investors), keeping funding for the sector strong in 2016 despite a general slowdown in other start-up areas.[46] The shift to industrial platforms is also an expression of national economic competition, as Germany (a traditional manufacturing power-house represented by Siemens) and the United States (a technology powerhouse represented by GE) are the primary supporters of this shift. Germany has enthusiastically bought into this idea and developed its own consortium to support the project, as has the United States, where companies like GE, Intel, Cisco, and IBM have partnered with the government in a similar non-profit con-sortium to push for smart manufacturing. At the moment the German consortium aims simply to raise awareness and support for the indus-trial Internet, while the American consortium is actively expanding trials with the technology.

The competition here is ultimately over the ability to build the monopolistic platform for manufacturing: 'It's winner takes all,' says GE's chief digital officer.[47] Predix and MindSphere both already offer infrastructural services (cloud-based computing), development tools, and applications for managing the industrial internet (i.e. an app store for factories). Rather than companies developing their own software to manage the internal internet, these platforms license out the tools needed. Expertise is necessary, for instance, in order to cope with the massive amounts of data that will be produced and to develop new analytical tools for things like time series data and geographical data. GE's liquid natural gas business alone is already collecting as many data as Facebook and requires a series of specialised tools to manage the influx of data.[48] The same holds for software designed to collect and analyse big data, for the modelling of physical-based systems, or for software that makes changes in factories and power plants. These platforms also provide the hardware (servers, storage, etc.) needed to operate an industrial internet. In competition with more generic platforms like AWS, industrial platforms promote themselves as having insider knowledge of manufacturing and the security necessary to run such a system. Like other platforms, these industrial firms rely on extracting data as a competitive tool against their rivals, a tool that ensures quicker, cheaper, more flexible services. By positioning themselves as the intermediary between factories, consumers, and app developers, these platforms are ideally placed to monitor much of how global manufacturing operates, from the smallest actuator to the largest factory, and they draw upon these data to further solidify their monopoly position. Deploying a standard platform strategy, both Siemens and GE also maintain openness in terms of who can connect to the platform, where data are stored (on site or in the cloud), and who can build apps for it. Network effects are, as always, essential to gaining a monopoly position, and this openness enables them to incorporate more and more users. These platforms already are strong revenue sources for the companies: Predix currently brings GE $5 billion and is expected to triple this revenue by 2020.[49] Predictions are that the sector will be worth $225 billion by 2020 – more than both the consumer internet of things and enterprise cloud computing.[50] Nevertheless, demonstrating the power of monopolies, GE continues to use AWS for its internal needs.[51]

Product Platforms

Importantly, the preceding developments – particularly the internet of things and cloud computing – have enabled a new type of on-demand platform. They are two closely related but distinct business models: the product platform and the lean platform. Take, for example, Uber and Zipcar – both platforms designed for consumers who wish to rent some asset for a time. While they are similar in this respect, their business models are significantly different. Zipcar owns the assets it rents out – the vehicles; Uber does not. The former is a product platform, while the latter is a lean platform that attempts to outsource nearly every possible cost. (Uber aims, however, eventually to command a fleet of self-driving cars, which would transform it into a product platform.) Zipcar, by contrast, might be considered a 'goods as a service' type of platform.

Product platforms are perhaps one of the biggest means by which companies attempt to recuperate the tendency to zero marginal costs in some goods. Music is the best example, as in the late 1990s downloading music for free became as simple as installing a small program. Record labels' revenues took a major dip, as consumers stopped purchasing compact discs (CDs) and other physical copies of music. Yet, in spite of its numerous obituaries, the music industry has been revived in recent years by platforms (Spotify, Pandora) that siphon off fees from music listeners, record labels, and advertisers alike. Between 2010 and 2014 subscription services have seen user numbers rise up from 8 million to 41 million, and subscription revenues are set to overtake download revenues as the highest source of digital music.[52] After years of decline, the music industry is poised to see its revenue grow once again in 2016. While subscription models have been around for centuries, for example in newspapers, what is novel today is their expansion to new realms: housing, cars, toothbrushes, razors, even private jets. Part of what has enabled these product platforms to flourish in recent years is the stagnation in wages and the decline in savings that we noted in Chapter 1. As less money is saved up, big-ticket purchases like cars and houses become nearly impossible and seemingly cheaper upfront fees appear more enticing. In the United Kingdom, for instance, household ownership has declined since 2008, while private rentals have skyrocketed.[53]

On-demand platforms are not affecting just software and consumer goods, though. One of the earliest stabs at an on-demand economy centred on manufactured goods, particularly durable goods. The most influential of these efforts was the transformation of the jet engine business from one that sold engines into one that rented thrust. The three big manufacturers – Rolls Royce, GE, and Pratt & Whitney – have all moved to this business model, with Rolls Royce leading the way in the late 1990s. The classic model of building an engine and then selling it to an airline was a relatively low margin business with high levels of competition. The competitive dynamics outlined in Chapter 1 are on full display here. Over the past 40 years the jet engine industry has been characterised by very few new companies, and no companies leaving the industry.[54] Instead the three major firms have competed intensely among themselves by introducing incremental technological improvements, in an effort to gain an edge. This technological competition continues today, when the jet engine industry pioneers the use of additive manufacturing. (For instance, GE's most popular jet engine has a number of parts that are now 3D printed rather than welded together out of different components.[55]) But margins on the engines themselves remain small, and competition tight. By contrast, the maintenance of these engines involves much higher profit margins – seven times higher, according to estimates.[56] The challenge with maintenance is that it is quite easy for outside competitors to come in to the market and take the profits away. This prompted Rolls Royce to introduce the 'goods as a service' model, whereby airlines do not purchase the jet engine but pay a fee for every hour one is used. In turn, Rolls Royce provides maintenance and replacement parts.

The raw material of data remains as central to this platform as to any other. Sensors are placed on all the engines and massive amounts of data are extracted from every flight, combined with weather data and information on air traffic control, and sent to a command centre in the United Kingdom. Information on the wear and tear on engines, possible problems, and times for scheduling maintenance are all derived. These data are immensely useful in blocking out competitors and in securing a competitive advantage against any outside maintenance firm that may hope to break into the market. Data on how the engines perform have also been crucial for developing new models: they enabled Rolls Royce to improve fuel efficiency and to increase the life of the engines, and generated another competitive advantage over other jet engine manufacturers. Once again, platforms appear as an optimal form for extracting data and using them to gain an edge over competitors. Data and the network effects of extracting them have enabled the company to establish dominance.

Lean Platforms

In the context of everything that has just been described, it is hard not to regard the new lean platforms as a retrogression to the earliest stages of the internet-enabled economy. Whereas the previous platforms have all developed business models that generate profits in some way, today's lean platforms have returned to the 'growth before profit' model of the 1990s. Companies like Uber and Airbnb have rapidly become household names and have come to epitomise this revived business model. These platforms range from specialised firms for a variety of services (cleaning, house calls from physicians, grocery shopping, plumbing, and so on) to more general marketplaces like TaskRabbit and Mechanical Turk, which provide a variety of services. All of them, however, attempt to establish themselves as the platform upon which users, customers, and workers can meet. Why are they 'lean' platforms? The answer lies in an oft-quoted observation: 'Uber, the world's largest taxi company, owns no vehicles […] and Airbnb, the largest accommodation provider, owns no property.'[57] It would seem that these are asset-less companies; we might call them virtual platforms.[58] Yet the key is that they do own the most important asset: the platform of software and data analytics. Lean platforms operate through a hyper-outsourced model, whereby workers are outsourced, fixed capital is outsourced, maintenance costs are outsourced, and training is outsourced. All that remains is a bare extractive minimum – control over the platform that enables a monopoly rent to be gained.

The most notorious part of these firms is their outsourcing of workers. In America, these platforms legally understand their workers as 'independent contractors' rather than 'employees'. This enables the companies to save around 30 per cent on labour costs by cutting out benefits, overtime, sick days, and other costs.[59] It also means outsourcing training costs, since training is only permitted for employees; and this process has led to alternatives forms of control via reputation systems, which often transmit the gendered and racist biases of society. Contractors are then paid by the task: a cut of every ride from Uber, of every rental from Airbnb, of every task fulfilled on Mechanical Turk. Given the reduction in labour costs provided by such an approach, it is no wonder that Marx wrote that the 'piece-wage is the form of wages most in harmony with the capitalist mode of production'.[60] Yet, as we have seen, this outsourcing of labour is part of a broader and longer outsourcing trend, which took hold in the 1970s. Jobs involving tradable goods were the first to be outsourced, while impersonal services were the next to go. In the 1990s Nike became a corporate ideal for contracting out, in that it contracted much of its labour to others. Rather than adopting vertical integration, Nike was premised upon the existence of a small core of designers and branders, who then outsourced the manufacturing of their goods to other companies. As a result, by 1996 people were already voicing concerns that we were transitioning to 'a "just-in-time" age of "disposable" workers'.[61] But the issue involves more than lean platforms. Apple, for instance, directly employs less than 10 per cent of the workers who contribute to the production of its products.[62] Likewise, a quick glance at the US Department of Labor can find a vast number of non-Uber cases involving the mislabelling of workers as independent contractors: cases related to construction workers, security guards, baristas, plumbers, and restaurant workers – to name just a few.[63] In fact the traditional labour market that most closely approximates the lean platform model is an old and low-tech one: the market of day labourers – agricultural workers, dock workers, or other low-wage workers – who would show up at a site in the morning in the hope of finding a job for the day. Likewise, a major reason why mobile phones have become essential in developing countries is that they are now indispensable in the process of finding work on informal labour markets.[64] The gig economy simply moves these sites online and adds a layer of pervasive surveillance. A tool of survival is being marketed by Silicon Valley as a tool of liberation.

We can also find this broader shift to non-traditional jobs in economic statistics. In 2005[65] the Bureau of Labour Statistics (BLS) found that nearly 15 million US workers (10.1 per cent of the labour force) were in alternative employment.[66] This category includes employees hired under alternative contract arrangements (on-call work, independent contractors) and employees hired through intermediaries (temp agencies, contract companies). By 2015 this category had grown to 15.8 per cent of the labour force.[67] Nearly half of this rise (2.5 per cent) was due to an increase in contracting out, as education, healthcare, and administration jobs were often at risk. Most strikingly, between 2005 and 2015, the US labour market added 9.1 million jobs – including 9.4 million alternative arrangement jobs. This means that the net increase in US jobs since 2005 has been solely from these sorts of (often precarious) positions.[68] Similar trends can be seen in self-employment. While the number of people who identify as self-employed has decreased, the number of people who filed the 1099 tax form for self-employment in the United States has increased.[69] What we see here is effectively an acceleration of the long-term tendency towards more precarious employment, particularly after 2008. The same trends are observable in the United Kingdom, where self-employment has created 66.5 per cent of net employment after

2008 and is the only thing that has staved off much higher levels of unemployment.[70]

Where do lean platforms fit into this? The most obvious point is the category of independent contractors and freelancers. This category has registered an increase of 1.7 per cent (2.9 million) between 2005 and 2015,[71] but most of these increases have been for offline work. Given that no direct measures of the sharing economy are currently available, surveys and other indirect measures have been used instead. Nearly all of the estimates suggest that around 1 per cent of the US labour force is involved in the online sharing economy formed by lean platforms.[72] Even here, the results have to take into account that Uber drivers probably form the majority of these workers.[73] The sharing economy outside of Uber is tiny. In the United Kingdom less evidence is presently available, but the most thorough survey done so far suggests that a slightly higher number of people routinely sell their labour through lean platforms. It is estimated that approximately 1.3 million UK workers (3.9 per cent of the labour force) work through them at least once a week, while other estimates range from 3 to 6 per cent of the labour force.[74] Other surveys suggest slightly higher numbers, but those problematically include a much larger range of activities.[75] What we can therefore conclude is that the sharing economy is but a small tip of a much larger trend. Moreover, it is a small sector, which is premised upon the vast growth in the levels of unemployment after the 2008 crisis. Building on the trends towards more precarious work that were outlined earlier, the crisis caused unemployment in the United States to double, while long-term unemployment nearly tripled. Moreover, the aftermath of the crisis was a jobless recovery – a phenomenon where economic growth returns, but job growth does not. As a result, numerous workers were forced to find whatever desperate means they could to survive. In this context, self-employment is not a freely chosen path, but rather a forced imposition. A look at the demographics of lean platform workers seems to support this. Of the workers on TaskRabbit, 70 per cent have Bachelor's degrees, while 5 per cent have PhDs.[76] An International Labour Organization (ILO) survey found that workers on Amazon's Mechanical Turk (AMT) also tend to be highly educated, 37 per cent using crowd work as their main job.[77] And Uber admits that around a third of its drivers in London come from neighbourhoods with unemployment rates of more than 10 per cent.[78] In a healthy economy these people would have no need to be micro-tasking, as they would have proper jobs.

While the other platform types have all developed novel elements, is there anything new about lean platforms? Given the broader context just outlined, we can see that they are simply extending earlier trends into new areas. Whereas outsourcing once primarily took place in manufacturing, administration, and hospitality, today it is extending to a range of new jobs: cabs, haircuts, stylists, cleaning, plumbing, painting, moving, content moderation, and so on. It is even pushing into white-collar jobs – copy-editing, programming and management, for instance. And, in terms of the labour market, lean platforms have turned what was once non-tradable services into tradable services, effectively expanding the labour supply to a near-global level. A multitude of novel tasks can now be carried out online through Mechanical Turk and similar platforms. This enables business, again, to cut costs by exploiting cheap labour in developing countries and places more downward pressure on wages by placing these jobs into global labour markets. The extent to which lean platform firms have outsourced other costs is also notable (though not novel); these are perhaps the purest attempts at a virtual platform to date. In doing so, these companies have been dependent upon the capacities offered by cloud platforms. Whereas firms once had to spend large amounts to invest in the computing equipment and expertise needed for their businesses, today's start-ups have flourished because they can simply rent hardware and software from the cloud. As a result, Airbnb, Slack, Uber, and many other start-ups use AWS.[79] Uber further relies on Google for mapping, Twilio for texting, SendGrid for emailing, and Braintree for payments: it is a lean platform built on other platforms. These companies have also offloaded costs from their balance sheets and shifted them to their workers: things like investment costs (accommodations for Airbnb, vehicles for Uber and Lyft), maintenance costs, insurance costs, and depreciation costs. Firms such as Instacart (which delivers groceries) have also outsourced delivery costs to food suppliers (e.g. Pepsi) and to retailers (e.g. Whole Foods) in return for advertising space.[80] However, even with this support,

Instacart remains unprofitable on 60 per cent of its business, and that is before the rather large costs of office space or the salaries of its core team are taken into account.[81] The lack of profitability has led to the predictable measure of cutting back on wages – a notably widespread phenomenon among lean platforms.

This has also prompted companies to compete on data extraction – again, a process optimised by the access afforded by platforms. Uber is perhaps the best example of this development, as it collects data on all of its rides, as well as data on drivers, even when they are not receiving a fare.[82] Data about what drivers are doing and how they are driving are used in a variety of ways in order to beat out competitors. For instance, Uber uses the data to ensure that its drivers are not working for other taxi platforms; and its routing algorithms use the data on traffic patterns to plot out the most efficient path for a trip. Data are fed into other algorithms to match passengers with nearby drivers, as well as to make predictions about where demand is likely to arise. In China, Uber monitors even whether drivers go to protests. All of this enables Uber to have a service that is quick and efficient from the passenger's point of view, thereby drawing users away from competitors. Data are one of the primary means of competition for lean platforms.

Nevertheless, these firms are still struggling to be profitable and the money to support them has to come from the outside. As we saw earlier, one of the important consequences of the 2008 crisis has been the intensification of an easy monetary policy and the growing corporate cash glut. The lean platform boom is, fundamentally, a post-2008 phenomenon. The growth of this sector is reflected most clearly in the number of deals made for start-up companies: VC deals have tripled since 2009.[83] Even after excluding Uber (which has an outsized position in the market), on-demand mobile services raised $1.7 billion over the course of 2014 – a 316 per cent increase from 2013.[84] And 2015 continued this trend towards more deals and higher volumes. But it is worth taking a moment to put the funding of lean platforms in context. When we look at the lean platforms for on-demand mobile services, we are primarily discussing Uber. In terms of funding, in 2014 Uber outpaced all the other service companies, taken together, by 39 per cent.[85] In 2015 Uber, Airbnb, and Uber's Chinese competitor,

Didi Chuxing, combined to take 59 per cent of all the funding for on-demand start-ups.[86] And, while the enthusiasm for new tech start-ups has reached a fever pitch, funding in 2015 ($59 billion) still paled in comparison to the highs of 2000 (nearly $100 billion).[87] Where is the money coming from? Broadly speaking, it is surplus capital seeking higher rates of return in a low interest rate environment. The low interest rates have depressed the returns on traditional financial investments, forcing investors to seek out new avenues for yield. Rather than a finance boom or a housing boom, surplus capital today appears to be building a technology boom. Such is the level of compulsion that even non-traditional funding from hedge funds, mutual funds, and investment banks is playing a major role in the tech boom. In fact, in the technology start-up sector, most investment financing comes from hedge funds and mutual funds.[88] Larger companies are also involved, Google being a major investor in the ill-fated Homejoy, while the logistics company DHL has created its own on-demand service MyWays, and firms like Intel and Google are also purchasing equity in a variety of new start-ups. Companies like Uber, deploying more than 135 subsidiary companies across the world, are also helped by tax evasion techniques.[89] Yet the profitability of these lean platforms remains largely unproven. Just like the earlier dot-com boom, growth in the lean platform sector is premised on expectations of future profits rather than on actual profits. The hope is that the low margin business of taxis will eventually pay off once Uber has gained a monopoly position. Until these firms reach monopoly status (and possibly even then), their profitability appears to be generated solely by the removal of costs and the lowering of wages and not by anything substantial.

In summary, lean platforms appear as the product of a few tendencies and moments: the tendencies towards outsourcing, surplus populations, and the digitisation of life, along with the post-2008 surge in unemployment and rise of an accommodative monetary policy, surplus capital, and cloud platforms that enable rapid scaling. While the lean model has garnered a large amount of hype and, in the case of Uber, a large amount of VC, there are few signs that it will inaugurate a major shift in advanced capitalist countries. In terms of outsourcing, the lean model remains a minor player in a long-term trend. The profit-making capacity of most lean models like-wise appears to be minimal and limited to a few specialised tasks. And, even there, the most successful of the lean models has been supported by VC welfare rather than by any meaningful revenue generation. Far from representing the future of work or that of the economy, these models seem likely to fall apart in the coming years.

Conclusion

We began this chapter by arguing that twenty-first-century capitalism has found a massive new raw material to appropriate: data. Through a series of developments, the platform has become an increasingly dominant way of organising businesses so as to monopolise these data, then extract, analyse, use, and sell them. The old business models of the Fordist era had only a rudimentary capacity to extract data from the production process or from customer usage. The era of lean production modified this slightly, as global 'just in time' supply chains demanded data about the status of inventories and the location of supplies. Yet data outside the firm remained nearly impossible to attain; and, even inside the firm, most of the activities went unrecorded. The platform, on the other hand, has data extraction built into its DNA, as a model that enables other services and goods and technologies to be built on top of it, as a model that demands more users in order to gain network effects, and as a digitally based medium that makes recording and storage simple. All of these characteristics make platforms a central model for extracting data as raw material to be used in various ways. As we have seen in this brief overview of some different platform types, data can be used in a variety of ways to generate revenues. For companies like Google and Facebook, data are, primarily, a resource that can be used to lure in advertisers and other interested parties. For firms like Rolls Royce and Uber, data are at the heart of beating the competition: they enable such firms to offer better products and services, control workers, and optimise their algorithms for a more competitive business. Likewise, platforms like AWS and Predix are oriented towards building (and owning) the basic infrastructures necessary to collect, analyse, and deploy data for other companies to use, and a rent is extracted for these platform services. In every case, collecting massive amounts of data is central to the business model and the platform provides the ideal extractive apparatus.

This new business form has intertwined with a series of long-term trends and short-term cyclical movements. The shift towards lean production and 'just in time' supply chains has been an ongoing process since the 1970s, and digital platforms continue it in heightened form today. The same goes for the trend towards outsourcing. Even companies that are not normally associated with outsourcing are still involved. For instance, content moderation for Google and Facebook is typically done in the Philippines, where an estimated 100,000 workers search through the content on social media and in cloud storage.[90] And Amazon has a notoriously low-paid workforce of warehouse workers who are subject to incredibly comprehensive systems of surveillance and control. These firms simply continue the secular trend of outsourcing low-skill workers while retaining a core of well-paid high-skill labourers. On a broader scale, all of the post-2008 net employment gains in America have come from workers in non-traditional employment, such as contractors and on-call workers. This process of outsourcing and building lean business models gets taken to an extreme in firms like Uber, which rely on a virtually asset-less form to generate profits. As we have seen, though, much of their profitability after the crisis has stemmed from holding wages down. Even the *Economist* is forced to admit that, since 2008, 'if the share of domestic gross earnings paid in wages were to rise back to the average level of the 1990s, the profits of American firms would drop by a fifth'.[91] An increasingly desperate surplus population has therefore provided a considerable supply of workers in low-wage, low-skill work. This group of exploitable workers has intersected with a vast amount of surplus capital set in a low interest rate world. Tax evasion, high corporate savings, and easy monetary policies have all combined, so that a large amount of capital seeks out returns in various ways. It is no surprise, then, that funding for tech start-ups has massively surged since 2010. Set in context, the lean platform economy ultimately appears as an outlet for surplus capital in an era of ultra-low interest rates and dire investment opportunities rather than the vanguard destined to revive capitalism.

While lean platforms seem to be a short-lived phenomenon, the other examples set out in this chapter seem to point to an important shift in how capitalist firms operate. Enabled by digital technology, platforms emerge as the means to lead and control industries. At their pinnacle, they have prominence over manufacturing, logistics, and design, by providing the basic landscape upon which the rest of the industry operates. They have enabled a shift from products to services in a variety of new industries, leading some to declare that the age of ownership is over. Let us be clear, though: this is not the end of ownership, but rather the concentration of ownership. Pieties about an 'age of access' are just empty rhetoric that obscures the realities of the situation. Likewise, while lean platforms have aimed to be virtually asset-less, the most significant platforms are all building large infrastructures and spending significant amounts of money to purchase other companies and to invest in their own capacities. Far from being mere owners of information, these companies are becoming owners of the infrastructures of society. Hence the monopolistic tendencies of these platforms must be taken into account in any analysis of their effects on the broader economy.

3

Great Platform Wars

If platforms are the emerging business model for the digital economy, how do they appear when set in the longer history of capitalism? In particular, up to this point we have largely left out one of the fundamental drivers of capitalism: intracapitalist competition. In Chapter 1 we set out the context of the long downturn – that period since the 1970s when the global economy has been saddled by overcapacity and overproduction in the manufacturing sector. As companies were unwilling and unable to destroy their fixed capital or to invest in new lines, international competition has steadily continued and, alongside it, the crisis of overcapacity in manufacturing. Unable to generate growth in this situation, in the 1990s the

United States began trying to stimulate the economy through an asset-price Keynesianism that operated by inducing low interest rates in order to generate higher asset prices and a wealth effect that would spark broader economic growth. This led to the dot-com boom of the 1990s and to the housing bubble of the early years of the twenty-first century. Today, as we saw in the previous chapter, asset-price Keynesianism continues apace and is one of the fundamental drivers behind the current mania for tech start-ups. Yet, behind the shiny new technology and slick façade of app interfaces, what broader consequences do these new firms hold for capitalism? In this chapter we will step back to look at the tendencies unleashed by these new firms into the broader economic environment of the long downturn. Some argue that capitalism renews itself through the creation and adoption of new technological complexes: steam and railways, steel and heavy engineering, automobiles and petrochemicals – and now information and communications technologies.[1] Are we witnessing the adoption of a new infrastructure that might revive capitalism's moribund growth? Will competition survive in the digital era, or are we headed for a new monopoly capitalism?

With network effects, a tendency towards monopolisation is built into the DNA of platforms: the more numerous the users who interact on a platform, the more valuable the entire platform becomes for each one of them. Network effects, moreover, tend to mean that early advantages become solidified as permanent positions of industry leadership. Platforms also have a unique ability to link together and consolidate multiple network effects. Uber, for instance, benefits from the network effects of more and more drivers as well as from the network effects of more and more riders.[2] Leading platforms tend consciously to perpetuate themselves in other ways as well. Advantages in data collection mean that the more activities a firm has access to, the more data it can extract and the more value it can generate from those data, and therefore the more activities it can gain access to. Equally, access to a multitude of data from different areas of our life makes prediction more useful, and this stimulates the centralisation of data within one platform. We give Google access to our email, our calendars, our video histories, our search histories, our locations – and, with each aspect provided to Google, we get better predictive services as a result. Likewise, platforms aim to facilitate complementary products: useful software built for Android leads more users to use Android, which leads more developers to develop for Android, and so on, in a virtuous circle. Platforms also seek to build up ecosystems of goods and services that close off competitors: apps that only work with Android, services that require Facebook logins. All these dynamics turn platforms into monopolies with centralised control over increasingly vast numbers of users and the data they generate. We can get a sense of how significant these monopolies already are by looking at how they consolidate ad revenue: in 2016 Facebook, Google, and Alibaba alone will take half of the world's digital advertising.[3] In the United States, Facebook and Google receive 76 per cent of online advertising revenue and are taking 85 per cent of every new advertising dollar.[4]

Yet it is also true that capitalism develops not only greater means for monopoly but also greater means for competition. The emergence of the corporation form, the rise of large financial institutions, and the monetary resources behind states all point to its capacity to initiate new lines of industry and to topple existing monopolies.[5] Equally importantly, digital platforms tend to arise in industries that are subject to disruption by new competitors.[6] Monopolies, in this view, should only ever be temporary. The challenge today, however, is that capital investment is not sufficient to overturn monopolies; access to data, network effects, and path dependency place even higher hurdles in the way of overcoming a monopoly like Google. This does not mean the end of competition or of the struggle for market power, but it means a change in the form of competition.[7] In particular, this is a shift away from competition over prices (e.g. many services are offered for free). Here we come to an essential point. Unlike in manufacturing, in platforms competitiveness is not judged solely by the criterion of a maximal difference between costs and prices; data collection and analysis also contribute to how competitiveness is judged and ranked. This means that, if these platforms wish to remain competitive, they must intensify their extraction, analysis, and control of data – and they must invest in the fixed capital to do so. And while their genetic drive is towards monopolisation, at present they are faced with an increasingly competitive environment comprised of other great platforms.

Tendencies

Since platforms are grounded upon the extraction of data and the generation of network effects, certain tendencies emerge from the competitive dynamics of these large platforms: expansion of extraction, positioning as a gatekeeper, convergence of markets, and enclosure of ecosystems. These tendencies then go on to be installed in our economic systems.

At one level, the expansion of platforms is driven by the cross-subsidisation of services used to draw users into a network. If a service appears likely to draw consumers or suppliers into the platform, then a company may develop the tools to do so. Yet expansion is also driven by factors other than user demand. One such factor is the drive for further data extraction. If collecting and analysing this raw material is the primary revenue source for these companies and gives them competitive advantages, there is an imperative to collect more and more. As one report notes, echoing colonialist ventures: 'From a data-production perspective, activities are like lands waiting to be discovered. Whoever gets there first and holds them gets their resources – in this case, their data riches.'[8] For many of these platforms, the quality of the data is of less interest than their quantity and diversity.[9] Every action performed by a user, no matter how minute, is useful for reconfiguring algorithms and optimising processes. Such is the importance of data that many companies could make all of their software open-source and still maintain their dominant position due to their data.[10] Unsurprisingly, then, these companies have been prolific purchasers and developers of assets that enable them to expand their capacity for gaining information. Mergers relating to big data, for instance, have doubled between 2008 and 2013.[11] Their vast cash glut and frequent use of tax havens contributed to making this possible. A large surplus of capital sitting idle has enabled these companies to build and expand an infrastructure of data extraction.

This is the context in which we should understand the significant investments made in the consumer internet of things (IoT), where sensors are placed in consumer goods and homes.[12] For example, Google's investment in Nest, a heating system for residential homes, makes much more sense when it is understood as the extension of data extraction. The same goes for Amazon's

new device, Echo, an always-on device that consumers place in their homes. At the mention of
its name, Echo will respond to questions; but
it is also capable of recording activities around
it. It is not difficult to see how this might be
useful for a company trying to understand consumer preferences. Similar devices already exist
in many phones – Siri for Apple, Google Now
for Android, not to mention the emergence of
smart TVs.[13] Wearable technologies are another
major element of consumer IoT. Nike, for
instance, is using wearables and fitness technology to bring users onto its platform and extract
their data. While all these devices may have
some use value for consumers, the field has not
been driven by consumers clamouring for them.
Instead, consumer IoT is only fully intelligible
as a platform-driven extension of data recording
into everyday activities. With consumer IoT, our
everyday behaviours start to be recorded: how we
drive, how many steps we take, how active we
are, what we say, where we go, and so on. This
is simply an expression of an innate tendency
within platforms. It is therefore no surprise that
one of Facebook's most recent acquisitions, the
Oculus Rift VR system, is able to collect all sorts

of data on its users and uses this information as part of the sales pitch to advertisers.[14]

The fact that the information platform requires an extension of sensors means that it is countering the tendency towards a lean platform. These are not asset-less companies – far from it; they spend billions of dollars to purchase fixed capital and take other companies over. Importantly, 'once we understand this [tendency], it becomes clear that demanding privacy from surveillance capitalists or lobbying for an end to commercial surveillance on the Internet is like asking Henry Ford to make each Model T by hand'.[15] Calls for privacy miss how the suppression of privacy is at the heart of this business model. This tendency involves constantly pressing against the limits of what is socially and legally acceptable in terms of data collection. For the most part, the strategy has been to collect data, then apologise and roll back programs if there is an uproar, rather than consulting with users beforehand.[16] This is why we will continue to see frequent uproars over the collection of data by these companies.

If data collection is a key task of platforms, analysis is the necessary correlate. The proliferation of data-generating devices creates a vast new repository of data, which requires increasingly large and sophisticated storage and analysis tools, further driving the centralisation of these platforms.[17] If expanding the capacity to collect data is one competitive imperative for these companies, developing corresponding means of analysis is another. Advances in hardware, database organisation, and network infrastructure therefore all play significant roles in gaining speed and insight advantages over one's competitors. Much of Google's initial success, for instance, stemmed from its pioneering work of creating useful internal software and innovative hardware architecture.[18] Rather uniquely, Google designs and builds its own custom servers rather than purchasing standard servers off the market – again, in an effort to gain competitive advantage.[19] And, while often it eventually releases information about its operations (which have then been copied by numerous others), it only does so after it has gained a clear advantage.[20] It is the importance of analytics that lets us understand why Google is heavily invested in artificial intelligence (AI) research as well, given that this is the key area for developing a competitive advantage over other platforms. Google is the biggest investor in this area, but Amazon, Salesforce, Facebook and Microsoft are all investing heavily in AI as well. Firms also have imperatives to develop the entire stack, and not just one area of it (e.g. data management, or analytical tools).[21] Bottlenecks in the flow of data from sensors to commodity are an impediment to producing more value. The result is a tendency to increasingly take on all the features of the stack, from hardware to software.

This is matched by a second tendency, whereby expansion across the ecosystem around a core business segment is driven in part by the need to occupy key positions within the ecosystem. These evade traditional distinctions: they are neither horizontal mergers (combining companies that directly compete), nor vertical mergers (combining companies within the same supply chain), nor conglomerate mergers (combining suppliers of similar and complementary products).[22] These mergers consist not so much in the vertical integration of classic Fordist firms or in the lean competencies of the post-Fordist era; they are more like rhizomatic connections driven by a permanent effort to place themselves in key platform positions. Let us take a first example. As access to the internet shifted away from desktop computing and towards handheld smartphones, control over the operating system (OS) platforms became essential. The shift caused companies to rush and implant themselves into the smartphone market: Google followed in Apple's footsteps, and Amazon and Facebook later attempted to catch up. Google used the traditional platform tactic of cross-subsidisation in order to occupy the mobile OS market: it licensed Android for free to hardware makers, so as to undercut Apple's enclosed system. The gambit worked, and Android today has more than 80 per cent of the market and is the most widely used OS on any device.[23] Similar competitive battles – and subsequent business expansions – have been going on at the interface level as well. As the primary means by which users interact with platforms, interfaces occupy a key intermediary position in the broader ecosystem. For the last decade, Google's search engine has been the primary interface into the rest of the internet, outpacing any other effort. Rival platforms have had to route around Google's search engine dominance by extending their business into new interface areas. One expression of this is that search engines within apps (rather than the open web) are becoming increasingly widespread. Instead of searching the internet through Google, users can search internally, on Amazon or Facebook. If people move into apps or start searching on Amazon instead of Google, these are threats to Google's basic business model.

Every major platform company is increasingly positioning itself in the natural language interface market as well. In 2016 Facebook began a major push for 'chatbots' – that is, low-level AI programmes that would converse with users on Facebook's platform. (This is also why Facebook – and numerous other companies – are investing heavily in AI and the natural language processing needed to enable chatbots.) The bet is that these chatbots will become the preferred way for users to interact with the internet. On this open platform, businesses would be given the tools to develop their own bots and create intuitive means for users to order food, buy a train ticket, or make a dinner reservation.[24] Rather than using a separate app or website for accessing businesses and services, users would simply access them through Facebook's platform, which would make

Facebook's chatbot platform the primary interface for commercial transactions online. Rather than trying to compete against Google's search engine or Amazon's logistics network, Facebook is trying to dominate the e-commerce platform by dominating the interface.

Whether this will work or not is debatable, but the principle is that these companies expand in intelligible ways, namely in order to take over key positions. Similar principles hold for Apple's, Google's, and Facebook's efforts to become a payment platform and to build the base for making economic transactions by collecting a small fee in every case, along with the data. This is also true of competition over mapping: Uber's bid to purchase a mapping provider, Google's use of Google Maps cars for its navigational basis, Apple's construction of its own locational services in 2012, and Uber's potential for building its own proprietary mapping provider. The aim is to occupy a position in the stack; where certain levels are more foundational and therefore more powerful, but also more difficult to secure and more subject to monopoly power and to major entry barriers. While we might think that being lower in the stack is correlated with greater power, this is not necessarily the case. Perhaps surprisingly, network providers (i.e. those that provide the basic telecommunications infrastructure) are in a low margin position in the ecosystem around platforms – a position that has compelled them to push for discriminatory pricing in moving data around (the end of 'net neutrality') as a way to generate more revenues.[25] The strategic importance of a position has much more to do with controlling data from businesses and customers than with just being lower in the stack.

These first two expansionary tendencies give platform monopolies a distinct path of expansion by comparison to traditional business models premised on vertical integration, horizontal integration, or conglomeration.[26] Instead, platform expansion is driven by the need for more data, which leads to what we might call the convergence thesis: the tendency for different platform companies to become increasingly similar as they encroach upon the same market and data areas. Currently there is a plethora of different platform models that have emerged from contingent economic conditions and strategic decisions based upon strengths in different areas.[27] One key question is what the future development of these forms holds: Will they converge into an ur-platform model? Or will they diverge and maintain competitiveness through specialisation? Given the need to expand data extraction and to position oneself in strategic locations, it would appear that companies are tendentially drawn into similar areas. This means that, despite their differences, companies like Facebook, Google, Microsoft, Amazon, Alibaba, Uber, and General Electric (GE) are also direct competitors. IBM, for instance, has moved into the platform business, purchasing Softlayer for cloud computing, and BlueMix for software development. The convergence thesis helps explain why Google is lobbying with Uber on self-driving cars and why Amazon and Microsoft have been discussing partnerships with German automakers on the cloud platform required by self-driving cars.[28] Alibaba and Apple have made major investments in Didi, Apple's partnership being particularly strategic, given that iPhones are the major interface to taxi services. And nearly all of the major platforms are working to develop medical data platforms. The trend to convergence is igniting international competition as well: intense struggles occur in India and China over who will dominate the ride-sharing industry (Uber, Didi, Lyft) and who will dominate e-commerce (Amazon, Alibaba, Flipkart). Alibaba is already the largest e-commerce site in the world as measured by the volume of its sales,[29] and Flipkart is valued at around $15 billion. Under the pressures of competition and the subsequent imperative to expand, we should expect these platforms to acquire as many companies as they need. Even second-tier platforms like Twitter and Yahoo are potential purchases, given the vast cash glut being held by the top tier of platforms (indeed, as I wrote this book, Microsoft purchased LinkedIn for $26 billion, gaining access to data on the changing interests, skills, and jobs of millions of workers). By 2015, global mergers and acquisitions had shot up more than 40 per cent above pre-crisis levels,[30] and the leading platforms have all made major moves in acquiring the resources needed to compete with their rivals. Ultimately, we see convergence – and therefore competition – across the field: smartphones, e-book readers, consumer IoT, cloud platforms, videochat services, payment services, driverless cars, drones, virtual reality, social networking, interfaces, network provision, search, and probably much more in the future.

A third dominant tendency is the funnelling of data extraction into siloed platforms. When extensive means are not sufficient for competitive advantage, this approach tries to tie users and data to the platform by locking them in through various measures: dependency on a service, inability to use alternatives, or lack of data portability, for instance. Apple is perhaps the leader in this tendency, as it makes its services and devices all highly interdependent and closed off to alternatives (with the notable exception of the semi-open App Store). Facebook is another clear example of this trend. Indeed, a major reason for Facebook's success is that, while Google dominated the open web through its search technology, Facebook was built as a closed platform that escaped the grips of Google. The aim for Facebook is to make it so that users never have to leave their enclosed ecosystem: news stories, videos, audio, messaging, email, and even buying consumer goods have all been progressively folded back into the platform itself. Enclosure takes on an even stricter form with Facebook's attempt to bring internet access to India and other countries through its Free

Basics program. Facebook's own services would be provided for free, but other services would have to partner with Facebook and go through its platform, effectively enclosing the entirety of the internet into Mark Zuckerberg's silo.[31] While rejected in India, the Free Basics service is now active in 37 countries and used by over 25 million people.[32] Uber is also effectively building up a system that funnels passengers into its system. The decreased demand for non-Uber cabs means a decreased supply of non-Uber drivers, as more and more of the services move onto Uber. As more passengers turn to Uber's platform, non-Uber cab drivers will lose out and be forced onto Uber's platform if they are to survive. The same holds for passengers: as fewer non-Uber cabs roam the streets, the only way to guarantee a cab will eventually be through Uber's platform. The field of industrial platform is also almost certain to resolve into a series of enclosed spaces, as Siemens and GE are unable (and unwilling) to communicate with each other. Manufacturers will be locked into whichever ecosystem they choose. This is particularly important in terms of intracapitalist competition: as non-platform companies are forced to use platforms to continue their business, a divide will grow between these two groups. Non-platform companies will put pressure on platforms to lower their prices, and platforms will fight back by making switching platforms increasingly costly and monopolistic. Amazon, too, aims to be a closed platform, separated from Google. Rather than turning to an internet search engine for buying goods online, users would search for goods, compare, purchase, track, and review, all without ever leaving the Amazon platform.

We also see the platform model driving the move from an open web to increasingly closed apps. The expansion of smartphones has led to more and more users interacting with the internet through apps rather than by visiting websites, and this is a way in which companies can both expand and close off data collection. As more users head into an app, those data are extracted there, while other platforms lose out. This trend also means that rivals seek to unmoor themselves from dependency on others: Dropbox is spending large amounts of money to separate itself from AWS, and Uber is seeking to untie itself from dependency on Google Maps. Even deeper down the stack, platforms are at work building their own network infrastructure. Google, for instance, has been building its own privatised internet – browsers, OSs, fibre networks, and data centres – where information may never have to journey across public infrastructure.[33] Likewise, Amazon's cloud network is nothing if not a private internet, and Microsoft and Facebook are collaborating to build their own transatlantic fibre cable.[34] Taken to a logical conclusion, this trend may lead to specialised platforms that give up on the idea of general computing and instead focus on optimising their particular services and the associated rents that go with these services.[35] In the end, the tendency of major platforms to grow to immense size thanks to network effects, combined with the tendency to converge towards a similar form, as market pressures dictate, leads them to use enclosure as a key means of competing against their rivals. If this analysis is right, then capitalist competition is driving the internet to fragment. There is no necessity to this outcome, as political efforts can stall or reverse it; but within a capitalist mode of production there are strong competitive pressures towards this end.

Challenges

For all the rhetoric of having overcome capitalism and of transitioning to a new mode of production – a rhetoric inherent in the postindustrial thesis of the 1960s, in the ideas of 'new economy' disciples in the 1990s, and in the radical and conservative paeans to the sharing economy of today – we still remain bound to a system of competition and profitability. Platforms offer new forms of competition and control, but in the end profitability is the great arbiter of success. Given these constraints, we must now open platforms up onto the wider economy. We can begin by returning to the scene of the long downturn and the problem of global manufacturing overcapacity. If we look to the US manufacturing sector, we find few signs that the sector is improving. In terms of output, manufacturing growth has dipped from an annual growth rate of 2.1 per cent between 1999 and 2008 to a rate of 1.3 per cent since.[36] Similar trends hold for labour productivity in the sector, which grew at a healthy 4.9 per cent annual rate between 1999 and 2008 but dropped to 1.9 per cent after the crisis.[37] This is perhaps to be expected, given the continued reliance of the US economy on the non-manufacturing sector's growth. But a broader global picture holds little hope either. Most notably, there is the massive overcapacity of manufacturing that China has built up. To take but one example, China is the main producer of steel in the world, responsible for over half of global production in 2015.[38] China currently requires about 700 million tonnes of steel domestically and 100 million tonnes for exports. Yet, despite continuing efforts to reduce its capacity, China is expected to still have a capacity for 1.1 billion tonnes of steel in 2020.[39] The result of overcapacity and overproduction has been the dumping of steel across the globe at very low prices, which drove down the prices in other countries and pushed companies like Tata Steel in Britain to the brink. The broader picture in China is even more dire. Estimates are that coal will soon have 3.3 billion tonnes of excess capacity, the aluminium industry is continuing to expand despite global oversupply, there may be 200 million tonnes of overcapacity in oil refining, and many chemical firms have been increasing their capacity despite running below potential output.[40] In this context, manufacturing firms are placing bets that the industrial internet will turn things around. Both Germany and America see this as a major opportunity – the former, to continue its position of dominance in high-value manufacturing, the latter, to revive its postwar position of dominance. The industrial internet will undoubtedly give rise to some successful firms who may be able for a time to derive extra profit, above and beyond what their competitors receive. The key question, though, is whether or not this in the long-term overcomes the lack of profitability and the overcapacity of global manufacturing. This seems unlikely, as nothing in the industrial internet program appears to radically transform manufacturing, but rather simply to reduce costs and downtime. Rather than improving productivity or developing new markets, the industrial internet appears to drive prices still further down and to increase the competition for market share, thereby exacerbating one of the main impediments to global growth. The platform owners will simply siphon off more of the revenue generated, leaving direct manufacturers with even less. On top of this, the widespread turn to austerity is continuing to depress aggregate demand across the world, and the global trends for productivity are in decline. Between 1999 and 2006 labour productivity grew by 2.6 per cent annually, but since the crisis the trend has been downwards to around 2.0 per cent.[41] Total factor productivity is even lower, at about zero per cent growth in the past few years – a trend that holds in nearly every major economy.[42]

In this context – given also the pushing down of short-term and long-term interest rates (into negative territory at points) – it is understandable that surplus capital would seek out returns wherever it can find them. Much like the 1990s boom, the start-up boom today appears to be driven largely by these forces: it is a continuation of asset-price Keynesianism rather than an abdication of its basic tenets. Yet there are other limits that prevent lean platforms from providing a sustainable source of dynamism. Perhaps the most pertinent limits are the ones involving outsourcing. The low margins of the business model indicate that services that rely on infrequent tasks (grocery shopping, home cleaning, etc.) are poised to suffer, as they simply do not generate frequent enough revenue to survive. Uber, rather uniquely, has the sweet spot, since so many people need to travel at any point in time. The evidence also suggests that high-skill personal jobs are unlikely to be successful on a lean platform, as they require training (and therefore employees) and they are subject to workers setting out on their own (rather than remaining in an exploitative relationship with a platform). Independent house cleaners, for instance, can often make more than the platforms can profitably offer, and this was ultimately one of the reasons why Homejoy collapsed.[43] Outsourcing to individual amateurs also means reducing the efficiencies that come with a large-scale professional service.[44] For instance, rather than Uber bulk-purchasing cabs for a fleet, individual drivers have to purchases vehicles. Or with Airbnb, rather than having a single professional cleaning staff, there are multiple amateur cleaners trying to accomplish the same tasks. Things like this mean that the overall costs are higher, which eventually threatens to make e-services more expensive and less productive than their traditional competitors. Some services that can draw upon a global labour force – small online tasks, data entry, content scrubbing, micro-programming, and so on – are likely to remain in business, simply because they draw upon hyper-exploited workers in low-income countries. For the most part, however, the attempt to outsource everything has overextended itself. This is even more pertinent as employee pushback against these firms is already occurring (there are Uber strikes and Uber unions, for instance), and these will inevitably raise the costs of operating these platforms. The calculations of one class action lawsuit estimate that Uber would owe its drivers $852 million if they were employees (Uber claims it would only be $429 million).[45] The result of pushback is likely to be an economically unsustainable business, once basic worker rights are given to employees.

Even with these advantages, there is a complete lack of profitability for most of these businesses. Numerous firms already have to cut costs and wages even further in order to give at least a plausible sense of potentially being profitable someday. The 'growth before profit' model dictates that taking significant losses is simply part of the strategy, though. Homejoy, a platform for housecleaning, attempted this by undercutting competitors with prices that were below costs, and eventually collapsed as a result.[46] Uber is perhaps the worst offender here, as it is reported to lose $1 billion a year only to fight off *another* unprofitable company in China.[47] It is hard to see a massive struggle between two unprofitable firms as representative of capitalism's leading light. Uber also spends an immense amount of money on lobbying and marketing, attempting to ensure favourable regulations and growth in its user base. Such is its desperation that Uber has even attempted to sabotage its competitors. It has made extensive use of this tactic in its dealings both with long-running cab companies and with alternative ride-sharing platforms. To fight off one competitor, for instance, Uber took to calling up and cancelling rides with its rival, in an effort to clog up that rival's supply of drivers.[48] When competition through data does not work, money and sabotage remain as options for lean platforms.

This leads us to the last major limit: lean platforms are entirely reliant on a vast mania of surplus capital. The investment in tech start-ups today is less an alternative to the centrality of finance and more an expression of it. Just like the original tech boom, it was initiated and sustained by a loose monetary policy and by large amounts of capital seeking higher returns. While it is impossible to call when a bubble may burst, there are signs that the enthusiasm for this sector is already over. Tech stocks have taken a massive hit in 2016.[49] There has been a wave of cutbacks on employee perks in the start-up sector – no more open bars and free snacks.[50] More significantly, growth in funding for US start-ups dropped drastically in the last quarter of 2015, by \$6 billion. With a sudden drop in venture capital funding, businesses are being forced to become profitable faster. For many low margin services, there are two options: either go out of business or cut costs and increase prices. What is likely to happen is for a large number of these services to go out of business in the next couple of years, while others will move towards becoming luxury services, providing on-demand convenience at high prices. Whereas the tech boom of the 1990s at least left us with the basis for the internet, the tech boom of the 2010s looks as though it will simply leave us with premium services for the rich.

While most of the other platform types appear to be in a strong enough position to weather any economic crisis and any blow to their business model, advertising platforms remain precariously dependent on ad revenues (e.g. Google at

89.0 per cent and Facebook at 96.6 per cent). It must also be recalled that platforms use cross-subsidisation to build their empires. Google's portfolio of free services and its investments in high technology are all built entirely on the back of profits made by its advertising services (and it is worth noting that finance is its largest ad customer).[51] Advertising is, under the capitalist valorisation process, a means to ensure that the value in commodities is realised through sales. It is an expression of competition between firms, but it does not itself produce new goods. Moreover, advertising is not exempt from economic crises. Between 2007 and 2012, spending on ads dropped by one half in Greece and by one third in Spain, while 2012 saw a 1.1 per cent drop in overall eurozone spending.[52] In the United States ad spending did not match 2008 levels until 2012.[53] More broadly, a long line of economic research shows that advertising is highly correlated with overall economic growth.[54] The low cost of digital advertising by comparison with traditional advertising has also meant that advertising growth has in recent years lagged behind economic growth, and is forecast to decrease even more in coming years.[55] It is simply cheaper than ever before to get the same amount of advertising. Problematically for Google and Facebook (and other ad-reliant services), the growth in digital advertising is expected to slow significantly, from an annual 14.7 per cent between 2009 and 2014 to 9.5 per cent from 2014 to 2019.[56] On top of all this, it is unclear whether advertising can thrive in a world of ad blockers, bots causing fake ad views, and routine spam. The global use of ad blockers grew 41 per cent in 2014 (when it prevented an estimated $21.8 billion dollars of advertising revenue) and 96 per cent in 2015.[57] By comparison, Facebook made $11.5 billion in advertising in 2014 – which means that ad blockers are not a minor issue for the industry. Companies are struggling against these technical trends – but one has to wonder whether society's wealth is best spent financing an advertising arms race. Meanwhile, new software is giving people more control over the data they make available, and governments around the world are beginning to regulate the collection of online data.[58] Advertising remains a precarious revenue stream for these companies. Even Google's chief economist, Hal Varian, expects that advertising will decline in importance and that Google will eventually move towards a pay-per-view model.[59]

If advertising declines – through some combination of economic crisis, ad blocking, and regulation – what will these platforms do? On the one hand, such a decline could accelerate the tendency towards enclosure. Ad blockers work on the open web, but in apps the platform has full control over what appears. For Google, as the interface of the open web, enclosure is not a possibility. This leaves the other option, as suggested by Varian: a shift towards direct payments of some form (rents, subscriptions, fees, micro-payments, etc.). There could be a move to the provision of essential platforms for other areas – a cut of every financial transaction, a licence fee for automakers to use Google's driverless platforms, a rent collected for every business that uses Google's cloud services. Or there could be a massive expansion of micro-payments, as the IoT enables every good to be turned into a service that charges by the use: cars, computers, doors, refrigerators, toilets.[60] Numerous businesses are already salivating over this option. In this context, companies like Rolls Royce, Uber, and GE may portend the future of platforms in any post-advertising environment. (Newspapers are currently grappling with a declining advertising stream; even *The New York Times* is forced to resort to services like meal delivery in order to gain revenue.)[61] On this option, rent is extracted from the use of a service and, given the monopoly position of these platforms, alternatives remain out of reach. Combined with stagnant wages and rising inequality, this future depicts a world with a massively increased digital divide. Finally, in the event of a major cutback on advertising, these platforms could be forced to cut back on all extravagant spending on long-shot ventures (drones, virtual reality, driverless cars, etc.), and to return to their core businesses. The cross-subsidisation of these ventures would come to an end, as would their ability to compete with other major platforms. In any case, the capitalist imperative to generate a profit means that these platforms will be forced either to develop novel means of extracting a surplus from the general economic pie or to fold their expansive cross-subsidising monopolies into much more traditional business forms.

Futures

What, then, does the future hold? If the tendencies set out in this book continue, we can expect one particular future. Platforms continue to expand across the economy, and competition drives them to enclose themselves increasingly. Platforms dependent on advertising revenues are compelled to transition more into direct payment businesses. Meanwhile lean platforms dependent on outsourcing costs and on venture capital largesse either go bankrupt or shift into product platforms (as Uber is attempting to do with driverless cars). In the end, it appears that platform capitalism has inbuilt tendencies to move towards extracting rents by providing services (in the form of cloud platforms, infrastructural platforms, or product platforms). In terms of profitability, Amazon is more the future than Google, Facebook, or Uber. In this scenario, the cross-subsidisation behind much of the internet's public-facing infrastructure would end, and existing inequalities in income and wealth would come to be replicated in access inequalities. Moreover, these platforms would come to siphon off large amounts of capital from the companies dependent upon them for their productive processes.

Some have argued that we might fight these monopolistic trends by building up cooperative platforms.[62] Yet all the traditional problems of coops (e.g. the necessity of self-exploitation under capitalist social relations) are made even worse by the monopolistic nature of platforms, the dominance of network effects, and the vast resources behind these companies. Even if all its software were made open-source, a platform like Facebook would still have the weight of its existing data, network effects, and financial resources to fight off any coop rival.

The state, by contrast, has the power to control platforms. Antitrust cases can break up monopolies, local regulations can impede or even ban exploitative lean platforms, government agencies can impose new privacy controls, and coordinated action on tax avoidance can draw capital back into public hands. These actions are perhaps all necessary, but we must admit that they remain rather unimaginative and minimal. They also neglect the structural conditions at play in the rise of platforms. In the midst of a long downturn in manufacturing, platforms have emerged as a way to siphon off capital into a relatively dynamic sector oriented towards the mining of data.

Rather than just regulating corporate platforms, efforts could be made to create public platforms – platforms owned and controlled by the people. (And, importantly, independent of the surveillance state apparatus.) This would mean investing the state's vast resources into the technology necessary to support these platforms and offering them as public utilities. More radically, we can push for postcapitalist platforms that make use of the data collected by these platforms in order to distribute resources, enable democratic participation, and generate further technological development. Perhaps today we must collectivise the platforms.

But any efforts to transform our condition must take the existence of platforms into account. Having a proper understanding of the current conjuncture is essential to creating strategies and tactics adequate to our moment. While platforms do not look set to overcome the fundamental conditions of the long downturn, they do appear to be consolidating monopoly power within their grasp, as they collect immense wealth.

As they reach out further and further into our digital infrastructure and as society becomes increasingly reliant upon them, it is crucial that we understand how they function and what can be done. Building a better future demands it.

Notes

Notes to Introduction

1 Morozov, 2015b.
2 Huws, 2014.
3 Since the phrase 'technology sector' is so often thrown around with little clarification, we will here define the sector using the North American Industry Classification System (NAICS) and its associated codes. Under that system, the tech sector can be considered to include computer and electronic product manufacturing (334), telecommunications (517), data processing, hosting, and related services (518), other information services (519), and computer systems design and related services (5415).
4 Klein, 2016.
5 Office for National Statistics, 2016b.
6 Davis, 2015: 7.

Notes to Chapter 1   The Long Downturn

1   Unless otherwise stated in the text, 'productivity' will refer to labour productivity rather than total factor productivity.

2   The following paragraph summarises Robert Brenner's insights in Brenner, 2007.

3   Braverman, 1999.

4   Piketty, 2014; Gordon, 2000; Glyn, Hughes, Lipietz, and Singh, 1990.

5   In many ways, this balance was the result of the defeat of radical labour and shop floor agitation rather than reflecting the success of the labour movement.

6   The following three paragraphs draw heavily on the account in Brenner, 2006.

7   Dyer-Witheford, 2015: 49–50.

8   Blinder, 2016.

9   Scheiber, 2015.

10 Brenner, 2002: 59–78, 128–33.

11 Antolin-Diaz, Drechsel, and Petrella, 2015; Bergeaud, Cette, and Lecat, 2015.

12 Perez, 2009; Goldfarb, Kirsch, and Miller, 2007: 115.

13 Goldfarb, Pfarrer, and Kirsch, 2005: 2.

14 Brenner, 2009: 21.

15 Perez, 2009.

16 Federal Reserve Bank of St Louis, 2016b.

17 *Comments of Verizon and Verizon Wireless*, 2010: 8n12.

18 Schiller, 2014: 80.

19 Dyer-Witheford, 2015: 82–4.

20 Greenspan, 1996.

21 Brenner, 2009: 23.

22 Rachel and Smith, 2015.

23 Khan, 2016.

24 The zero lower bound, or liquidity trap, argues that nominal interest rates cannot go below zero (otherwise savers would take their money out and put it under the proverbial mattress). The result is that policymakers cannot push nominal interest rates below zero. For more, see Krugman, 1998. Recently some countries have begun imposing negative rates on reserves held at the central bank, though the effects of this action appear so far to be minimal and possibly contrary to what is intended (e.g. decreasing lending, rather than increasing lending).

25 Khan, 2016.

26 Joyce, Tong, and Woods, 2011; Gagnon, Raskin, Remache, and Sack, 2011; Bernanke, 2012: 7.

27 Dobbs, Lund, Woetzel, and Mutafchieva, 2015: 8.

28 Spross, 2016.

29 Karabarbounis and Neiman, 2012.

30 Reserves refers to their holdings of cash, cash equivalents, and marketable securities.

31 Zucman, 2015: 46.

32 Ibid., 35. Notably this estimate excludes banknotes (estimated around $400 billion) and physical assets like art, jewellery, and real estate, which are also used to avoid taxes.

33 Srnicek and Williams, 2015: ch. 5.

34 Federal Reserve Bank of St Louis. 2016a.

35 Office for National Statistics, 2016b.

Notes to Chapter 2   Platform Capitalism

1 Löffler and Tschiesner, 2013.
2 Kaminska, 2016a.
3 Vercellone, 2007.
4 Terranova, 2000.
5 Wark, 2004.
6 Author's calculation on the basis of data from Andrae and Corcoran, 2013 and US Energy Information Administration, n.d.; for more, see Maxwell and Miller, 2012.
7 One particularly illuminating example of this comes from climate science; see Edwards, 2010.
8 I draw here upon Marx's definition of raw material: 'The land (and this, economically speaking, includes water) in the virgin state in which it supplies man with necessaries or the means of subsistence ready to hand, exists independently of him, and is the universal subject of human labour. All those things which labour merely separates from immediate connexion with their environment, are subjects of labour spontaneously provided by Nature. Such are fish which we catch and take from their element, water, timber which we fell in the virgin forest, and ores which we extract from their veins. *If, on the other hand, the subject of labour has, so to say, been filtered through previous labour, we call it raw material*; such is ore already extracted and ready for washing' (Marx, 1990: 284–5, emphasis added).
9 A useful relation could perhaps be drawn to Jason Moore's concept of cheap inputs, although this lies

outside the scope of this study; see ch. 2 in Moore, 2015.

10 Apple is one example of a major company excluded by this focus, as it is primarily a traditional consumer electronics producer with now standard practices of outsourcing manufacturing. It has some platform elements to its business (iTunes, the App Store), but these only generate 8.0 per cent of the revenues that Apple is famous for. The vast majority (68.0 per cent) of revenues come from iPhone sales. Apple is more akin to the 1990s Nike business model than to the 2010s Google business model.

11 For useful complementary approaches to platforms, see Bratton, 2015: ch. 9 and Rochet and Tirole, 2003.

12 While technically platforms can exist in non-digital forms (e.g. a shopping mall), the ease of recording activities online makes digital platforms the ideal model for data extraction in today's economy.

13 By 'user' we also include machines – an important addition when considering the internet of things. See: Bratton, 2015: 251–89.

14 Gawer, 2009: 54.

15 Rochet and Tirole, 2003.

16 Kaminska, 2016b.

17 Hwang and Elish, 2015.

18 Metz, 2012.

19 We can imagine a scenario where a firm owns the code of a platform but rents all of its computing needs from a cloud-based service. Hardware is therefore not essential to the ownership of a platform. But, given the

competitive demands that we will outline later on, the largest platforms have all moved towards proprietary hardware. In other words, ownership of fixed capital remains important to these firms, if not essential.

20 Goldfarb, Kirsch, and Miller, 2007: 128.
21 Crain, 2014: 377–8.
22 Zuboff, 2016.
23 Varian, 2009.
24 Terranova, 2000.
25 Wittel, 2016: 86.
26 Zuboff, 2015: 78.
27 Ibid.
28 For one example of a data value chain, see Dumbill, 2014.
29 Finnegan, 2014.
30 Davidson, 2016.
31 CB Insights, 2016b.
32 Henwood, 2003: 30.
33 Hook, 2016.
34 Clark and Young, 2013.
35 Burrington, 2016.
36 In the industry, these are known respectively as 'infrastructure as a service' (IaaS), 'platform as a service' (Paas), and 'software as a service' (SaaS).
37 Clark, 2016.
38 Miller, 2016.
39 Asay, 2015.
40 McBride and Medhora, 2016.
41 Webb, 2015; Bughin, Chui, and Manyika, 2015.
42 Bughin, Chui, and Manyika, 2015.
43 Alessi, 2014.

44 World Economic Forum, 2015: 4.

45 Zaske, 2015.

46 CB Insights, 2016c.

47 Waters, 2016.

48 Murray, 2016.

49 Miller, 2015b.

50 Waters, 2016.

51 Miller, 2015a.

52 International Federation of the Phonographic Industry, 2015: 6–7.

53 Office for National Statistics, 2016a.

54 Bonaccorsi and Giuri, 2000: 16–21.

55 Dishman, 2015.

56 'Britain's Lonely High-Flier', 2009.

57 Goodwin, 2015.

58 Incidentally, they appear to be owned by what McKenzie Wark calls the vectoralist class; see Wark, 2004.

59 Kamdar, 2016; Kosoff, 2015.

60 Marx, 1990: 697–8.

61 Polivka, 1996: 3.

62 Scheiber, 2015.

63 US Department of Labor, n.d.

64 Dyer-Witheford, 2015: 112–14.

65 The BLS measures the gig economy indirectly, through 'contingent and alternative employment' – but stopped in 2005, after funding was cut. They are, however, set to carry out another survey in 2017; see BLS Commissioner, 2016.

66 US Department of Labor, 2005: 17.

67 This estimate is based on an attempt to duplicate

the BLS surveys as closely as possible. See Katz and Krueger, 2016.

68 Ibid.

69 Wile, 2016.

70 Office for National Statistics, 2014: 3.

71 Katz and Krueger, 2016.

72 Various estimates include: 0.5% of the labour force (Katz and Kreuger, 2016); 0.4–1.3% (Harris and Kreuger, 2015: 12); 1.0% (McKinsey: see Manyika, Lund, Robinson, Valentino, and Dobbs, 2015); 2.0% (Intuit: see Business Wire, 2015). One outlier survey from Burson-Marsteller suggests that 28.6% of the US labour force has provided services through the gig economy (see Burson-Marsteller, Aspen Institute, and TIME, 2016).

73 Harris and Krueger, 2015: 12.

74 Various estimates are: 3.0% of the labour force (Coyle, 2016: 7); 3.9% (Huws and Joyce, 2016); 6.0% (Business Wire, 2015). See also Hesse, 2015.

75 A Nesta survey found that 25% of Brits had been involved in internet-enabled collaborative activity, but this category includes people who purchase from the internet rather than just workers. It also includes people who donate goods or purchase media online. An Intuit survey, on the other hand, reportedly found that 6% of the population in Britain is working in the sharing economy, but the actual data do not appear to be available. See Stokes, Clarence, Anderson, and Rinne, 2014: 25; Hesse, 2015.

76 Henwood, 2015.

77 Berg, 2016.

78 Knight, 2016.
79 See many more examples at Amazon Web Services, 2016.
80 Huet, 2016.
81 Ibid.
82 While government surveillance is often the focus of public attention today, corporate surveillance is just as pernicious a phenomenon. Pasquale, 2015.
83 'Reinventing the Deal', 2015.
84 CB Insights, 2015.
85 Ibid.
86 CB Insights, 2016a.
87 National Venture Capital Association, 2016: 9; Crain, 2014: 374.
88 CB Insights, 2016d.
89 O'Keefe and Jones, 2015.
90 Chen, 2014.
91 'The Age of the Torporation', 2015.

Notes to Chapter 3   Great Platform Wars

1 Perez, 2009: 782.
2 MIT Technolosgy Review, 2016: 7.
3 See Burson-Marsteller, 2016.
4 Meeker, 2016; Herrman, 2016.
5 Brenner and Glick, 1991: 89.
6 This is the justification that the United Kingdom's House of Lords gives for claiming that monopolies in platforms are not a major concern. Select Committee on European Union, 2016.
7 Wheelock, 1983; Baran and Sweezy, 1966: 76.

8 MIT Technology Review, 2016: 6.
9 Zuboff, 2015: 79.
10 Stucke and Grunes, 2016: 45.
11 Ibid., 40.
12 Curiously, the first 'internet of things' was a toaster that was connected to and controlled by the internet in 1989.
13 Kelion, 2013.
14 Mason, 2016.
15 Zuboff, 2016.
16 Zuboff, 2015: 79–80.
17 Bratton, 2015: 116.
18 Metz, 2012.
19 Shankland, 2009.
20 Metz, 2012.
21 MIT Technology Review, 2016: 8.
22 Stucke and Grunes, 2016: 127–8.
23 Bradshaw, 2016.
24 Kuang, 2016.
25 Schiller, 2014: 91–3.
26 Stucke and Grunes, 2016: 106.
27 Bratton, 2015: 142.
28 Taylor, 2016.
29 World Bank, 2016: 109.
30 Kawa, 2016.
31 Morozov, 2015a: 56.
32 Bowles, 2016.
33 Bratton, 2015: 118.
34 Lardinois, 2016.
35 Ibid., 119.
36 US Department of Labor, 2016a.

37 US Department of Labor, 2016b.
38 Word Steel Association, 2016.
39 Mitchell, 2016.
40 'Gluts for Punishment', 2016.
41 The Conference Board, 2015: 4.
42 Ibid., 5.
43 Farr, 2015.
44 Kaminska, 2016c.
45 Levine and Somerville, 2016.
46 Farr, 2015.
47 Jourdan and Ruwitch, 2016.
48 Biddle, 2014.
49 Shinal, 2016.
50 Kim, 2016.
51 WordStream, 2011.
52 Bradshaw, 2012.
53 Vega and Elliott, 2011.
54 Jones, 1985; Chang and Chan-Olmsted, 2005; van der Wurff, Bakker, and Picard, 2008.
55 McKinsey & Company, 2015: 7, 11.
56 Ibid., 17.
57 'The Cost of Ad Blocking', 2016: 3; Meeker, 2016.
58 Pollack, 2016.
59 Varian, 2015.
60 Morozov, 2016.
61 Smith, 2016.
62 Scholz, 2015.

References

'The Age of the Torporation'. 2015. *The Economist*, 24 October. http://www.economist.com/news/business/21676803-big-listed-firms-earnings-have-hit-wall-deflation-and-stagnation-age-torporation (accessed 4 June 2015).

Alessi, Christopher. 2014. 'Germany Develops "Smart Factories" to Keep an Edge'. *MarketWatch*, 27 October. http://www.marketwatch.com/story/germany-develops-smart-factories-to-keep-an-edge-2014-10-27 (accessed 2 June 2016).

Amazon Web Services. 2016. 'Case Studies and Customer Success Stories, Powered by the AWS Cloud'. https://aws.amazon.com/solutions/case-studies (accessed 12 June 2016).

Andrae, Anders, and Peter Corcoran. 2013. 'Emerging

Trends in Electricity Consumption for Consumer ICT'. NUI Galway. https://aran.library.nuigalway.ie/handle/10379/3563 (accessed 2 June 2016).

Antolin-Diaz, Juan, Thomas Drechsel, and Ivan Petrella. 2015. 'Following the Trend: Tracking GDP When Long-Run Growth Is Uncertain'. Fulcrum. https://www.fulcrumasset.com/Research/ResearchPapers/2015-09-25/Following-the-Trend-Tracking-GDP-when-lon grun-growth-is-uncertain (accessed 2 June 2016).

Asay, Matt. 2015. 'Amazon's Cloud Business Is Worth At Least $70 Billion'. *ReadWrite*, 23 October. http://readwrite.com/2015/10/23/aws-amazon-cloud (accessed 2 June 2016).

Baldwin, Carliss, and C. Jason Woodard. 2009. 'The Architecture of Platforms: A Unified View'. In *Platforms, Markets and Innovation*, edited by Annabelle Gawer, pp. 19–44. Cheltenham: Edward Elgar.

Baran, Paul, and Paul Sweezy. 1966. *Monopoly Capital: An Essay on the American Economic and Social Order*. Harmondsworth: Penguin Books.

Berg, Janine. 2016. 'Highlights from an ILO Survey of Crowdworkers'. Paper presented at the Workshop on the Measurement of Digital Work, Brussels, 18 February. http://dynamicsofvirtualwork.com/wp-content/uploads/2016/03/Berg-presentation.pdf (accessed 2 June 2016).

Bergeaud, Antonin, Gilbert Cette, and Rémy Lecat. 2015. 'Productivity Trends in Advanced Countries between 1890 and 2012'. *Review of Income and Wealth*. doi: 10.1111/roiw.12185.

Bernanke, Ben. 2012. 'Monetary Policy since the Onset of the Crisis'. Paper presented at the Federal Reserve Bank of Kansas City Economic Symposium, Jackson Hole, Wyoming, 31 August. https://www.federalreserve.gov/newsevents/speech/bernanke20120831a.htm (accessed 2 June 2016).

Biddle, Sam. 2014. 'Uber's Dirty Trick Campaign Against NYC Competition Came From the Top'. *Valleywag*, 24 January. http://valleywag.gawker.com/ubers-dirty-trick-campaign-against-nyc-competition-cam-1508280668 (accessed 2 June 2016).

Blinder, Alan. 2016. 'Offshoring: The Next Industrial Revolution?' *Foreign Affairs*, March–April. https://www.foreignaffairs.com/articles/2006-03-01/offshoring-next-industrial-revolution (accessed 2 June 2016).

BLS Commissioner. 2016. 'Why This Counts: Measuring "Gig" Work'. *Commissioner's Corner*, 3 March. http://blogs.bls.gov/blog/2016/03/03/

why-this-counts-measuring-gig-work (accessed 2 June 2016).

Bonaccorsi, Andrea, and Paola Giuri. 2000. 'Industry Life Cycle and the Evolution of an Industry Network'. LEM Working Papers Series, Laboratory of Economics and Management (LEM), Sant'Anna School of Advanced Studies, Pisa. http://www.lem.sssup.it/WPLem/files/2000-04.pdf (accessed 2 June 2016).

Bowles, Nellie. 2016. 'Facebook's "Colonial" Free Basics Reaches 25 Million People – Despite Hiccups'. *The Guardian*, 12 April 12. http://www.theguardian.com/technology/2016/apr/12/facebook-free-basics-program-reach-f8-developer-conference (accessed 2 June 2016).

Bradshaw, Tim. 2012. 'European Advertising Spending Off Target'. *Financial Times*, 19 June. http://www.ft.com/cms/s/0/5585ecc8-b964-11e1-a470-00144feabdco.html (accessed 30 June 2016).

Bradshaw, Tim. 2016. 'How Tiny Android Became a Giant in the Smartphone Galaxy'. *Financial Times*, 20 April. http://www.ft.com/cms/s/0/9271f24c-0714-11e6-9b51-0fb5e65703ce.html#axzz4BoRCjtDo (accessed 2 June 2016).

Bratton, Benjamin. 2015. *The Stack: On Software and Sovereignty*. Cambridge, MA: MIT Press.

Braverman, Harry. 1999. *Labor and Monopoly Capitalism: The Degradation of Work in the Twentieth Century* (25th anniversary edn). New York: Monthly Review Press.

Brenner, Robert. 2002. *The Boom and the Bubble: The US in the World Economy*. London: Verso.

Brenner, Robert. 2006. *The Economics of Global Turbulence*. London: Verso.

Brenner, Robert. 2007. 'Property and Progress: Where Adam Smith Went Wrong'. In *Marxist History-Writing for the Twenty-First Century*, edited by Chris Wickham, pp. 49–111. Oxford: Oxford University Press.

Brenner, Robert. 2009. 'What Is Good for Goldman Sachs Is Good for America: The Origins of the Present Crisis', pp. 1–73. e-Scholaship, Center for Social Theory and Comparative History, UCLA, 2 October. http://escholarship.org/uc/item/0sg0782h (accessed 7 June 2016).

Brenner, Robert, and Mark Glick. 1991. 'The Regulation Approach: Theory and History'. *New Left Review*, 188: 45–119.

'Britain's Lonely High-Flier' (Editor's Note). 2009. *The Economist*, 8 January. http://www.economist.com/node/12887368 (accessed 4 June 2016).

Bughin, Jacques, Michael Chui, and James Manyika.

2015. 'An Executive's Guide to the Internet of Things'. McKinsey&Company. August. http://www. mckinsey.com/business-functions/business-technology/our-insights/an-executives-guide-to-the-internet-of-things (accessed 4 June 2016).

Burrington, Ingrid. 2016. 'Why Amazon's Data Centers Are Hidden in Spy Country'. *The Atlantic*, 8 January. http://www.theatlantic.com/technology/archive/2016/01/amazon-web-services-data-center/423147 (accessed 4 June 2016).

Burson-Marsteller. 2016. 'Net Display Ad Revenues Worldwide, by Company, 2014–2016'. https://pbs.twimg.com/media/Chsi8ZwUgAA-NnG.jpg (accessed 4 June 2016).

Burson-Marsteller, Aspen Institute, and TIME. 2016. *The On-Demand Economy Survey*. Burson-Marsteller. 6 January. http://www.burson-marsteller.com/ondemand-survey (accessed 5 June 2016).

Business Wire. 2015. 'Intuit Forecast: 7.6 Million People in On-Demand Economy by 2020'. Business Wire. 13 August. http://www.businesswire.com/news/home/20150813005317/en (accessed 27 May 2016).

CB Insights. 2015. 'The On-Demand Report' (homepage). https://www.cbinsights.com/research-on-demand-report (accessed 5 June 2016).

CB Insights. 2016a. 'Just 3 Unicorn Startups Take the Majority of On-Demand Funding in 2015'. 3 March. https://www.cbinsights.com/blog/on-demand-funding-top-companies (accessed 27 May 2016).

CB Insights. 2016b. 'Microsoft Races Ahead with M&A as Yahoo, Google and Others Pull Back'. 4 March. https://www.cbinsights.com/blog/top-tech-companies-acquisition-trends (accessed 22 May 2016).

CB Insights. 2016c. 'The New Manufacturing: Funding to Industrial IoT Startups Jumps 83% in 2015'. 3 March. https://www.cbinsights.com/blog/industrial-iiot-funding (accessed 5 June 2016).

CB Insights. 2016d. 'Tech IPO Report' (homepage). https://www.cbinsights.com/research-tech-ipo-report-2016 (accessed 12 June 2016).

Chang, Byeng-Hee, and Sylvia M. Chan-Olmsted. 2005. 'Relative Constancy of Advertising Spending: A Cross-National Examination of Advertising Expenditures and Their Determinants'. *International Communication Gazette*, 67 (4): 339–57.

Chen, Adrian. 2014. 'The Laborers Who Keep Dick Pics and Beheadings Out of Your Facebook Feed'. *Wired*, 23 October. http://www.wired.com/2014/10/content-moderation (accessed 4 June 2016).

Clark, Jack. 2016. 'Google Taps Machine Learning to Lure Companies to Its Cloud'. Bloomberg Technology. 23 March. http://www.bloomberg.com/news/articles/2016-03-23/google-taps-machine-learning-to-lure-companies-to-its-cloud (accessed 4 June 2016).

Clark, Meagan, and Angelo Young. 2013. 'Amazon: Nearly 20 Years in Business and It Still Doesn't Make Money, but Investors Don't Seem to Care'. *International Business Times*, 18 December. http://www.ibtimes.com/amazon-nearly-20-years-business-it-still-doesnt-make-money-investors-dont-seem-care-1513368 (accessed 4 June 2016).

Comments of Verizon and Verizon Wireless. 2010. Department of Commerce, 6 December. https://www.ntia.doc.gov/files/ntia/comments/100921457-0457-01/attachments/12%2006%2010%20VZ,%20VZW%20comments_Global%20Internet.pdf (accessed 4 June 2016).

The Conference Board. 2015. 'Productivity Brief 2015: Global Productivity Growth Stuck in the Slow Lane with No Signs of Recovery in Sight'. The Conference Board, New York. https://www.conference-board.org/retrievefile.cfm?filename=The-Conference-Board-2015-Productivity-Brief.pdf&type=subsite (accessed 25 May 2016).

'The Cost of Ad Blocking'. 2016. PageFair and Adobe. https://downloads.pagefair.com/wp-content/uploads/2016/05/2015_report-the_cost_of_ad_blocking.pdf (accessed 4 June 2016).

Coyle, Diane. 2016. *The Sharing Economy in the UK*. London: Sharing Economy UK. http://www.sharingeconomyuk.com/perch/resources/210116thesharingeconomyintheuktpdc.docxIIII.docx-2.pdf (accessed 1 June 2016).

Crain, Matthew. 2014. 'Financial Markets and Online Advertising: Reevaluating the Dotcom Investment Bubble'. *Information, Communication & Society*, 17 (3): 371–84.

Davidson, Adam. 2016. 'Why Are Corporations Hoarding Trillions?' *The New York Times*, 20 January. http://www.nytimes.com/2016/01/24/magazine/why-are-corporations-hoarding-trillions.html (accessed 29 May 2016).

Davis, Jerry. 2015. 'Capital Markets and Job Creation in the 21st Century'. Brookings Institution, Washington, DC. http://www.brookings.edu/~/media/research/files/papers/2015/12/30-21st-century-job-creation-davis/capital_markets.pdf (accessed 29 May 2016).

Dishman, Lydia. 2015. 'Thrust for Sale: Innovation Takes Flight'. GE Digital, 10 June. https://www.

ge.com/digital/blog/thrust-sale-innovation-takes-flight (accessed 29 May 2016).

Dobbs, Richard, Susan Lund, Jonathan Woetzel, and Mina Mutafchieva. 2015. 'Debt and (Not Much) Deleveraging'. McKinsey Global Institute. http://www.mckinsey.com/global-themes/employment-and-growth/debt-and-not-much-deleveraging#st_refDomain=&st_refQuery= (accessed 29 May 2016).

Dumbill, Edd. 2014. 'Understanding the Data Value Chain'. IBM Big Data & Analytics Hub. 10 November. http://www.ibmbigdatahub.com/blog/understanding-data-value-chain (accessed 29 May 2016).

Dyer-Witheford, Nick. 2015. *Cyber-Proletariat: Global Labour in the Digital Vortex*. London: Pluto Press.

Edwards, Paul. 2010. *A Vast Machine: Computer Models, Climate Data, and the Politics of Global Warming*. Cambridge, MA: MIT Press.

Farr, Christina. 2015. 'Homejoy at the Unicorn Glue Factory'. *Backchannel*. 26 October. https://backchannel.com/why-homejoy-failed-bb0ab39d901a (accessed 25 May 2016).

Federal Reserve Bank of St Louis. 2016a. Personal Saving Rate. https://research.stlouisfed.

org/fred2/series/PSAVERT (accessed 12 June 2016).

Federal Reserve Bank of St Louis. 2016b. 'Private fixed investment: Nonresidential: Information processing equipment and software: Computers and peripheral equipment'. Economic Research. https://research.stlouisfed.org/fred2/series/B935RC1Q027SBEA (accessed 12 June 2016).

Finnegan, Matthew. 2014. 'Wearables Health Data "Massive Opportunity" for Retailers, Says Dunnhumby CIO'. Computerworld UK, 2 October. http://www.computerworlduk.com/it-management/wearables-health-data-massive-opportunity-for-retailers-dunnhumby-cio-3574885 (accessed 25 May 2016).

Gagnon, Joseph, Matthew Raskin, Julie Remache, and Brian Sack. 2011. 'The Financial Market Effects of the Federal Reserve's Large-Scale Asset Purchases'. *International Journal of Central Banking*, 7 (1): 3–43.

Gawer, Annabelle. 2009. 'Platform Dynamics and Strategies: From Products to Services'. In *Platforms, Markets and Innovation*, edited by Annabelle Gawer, pp. 45–76. Cheltenham: Edward Elgar.

'Gluts for Punishment'. 2016. *The Economist*, 9 April. http://www.economist.com/news/business/

21696552-chinas-industrial-excess-goes-beyond-steel-gluts-punishment (accessed 25 May 2016).

Glyn, Andrew, Alan Hughes, Alain Lipietz, and Ajit Singh. 'The Rise and Fall of the Golden Age'. 1990. In *The Golden Age of Capitalism: Reinterpreting the Postwar Experience*, edited by Stephen Marglin and Juliet Schor, pp. 39–125. Oxford: Oxford University Press.

Goldfarb, Brent, David Kirsch, and David A. Miller. 2007. 'Was There Too Little Entry During the Dot Com Era?' *Journal of Financial Economics*, 86 (1): 100–44.

Goldfarb, Brent, Michael Pfarrer, and David Kirsch. 2005. 'Searching for Ghosts: Business Survival, Unmeasured Entrepreneurial Activity and Private Equity Investment in the Dot-Com Era'. Working Paper RHS-06-027. Social Science Research Network, Rochester. SSRN-id929845, downloadable at http://papers.ssrn.com/abstract=825687 (accessed 25 May 2016).

Goodwin, Tom. 2015. 'The Battle Is for the Customer Interface'. *TechCrunch*. 3 March. http://social.techcrunch.com/2015/03/03/in-the-age-of-disintermediation-the-battle-is-all-for-the-customer-interface (accessed 25 May 2016).

Gordon, Robert. 2000. 'Interpreting the "One Big

Wave" in US Long-Term Productivity Growth'. NBER Working Paper 7752. National Bureau of Economic Research. http://www.nber.org/papers/w7752 (accessed 25 May 2016).

Greenspan, Alan. 1996. 'The Challenge of Central Banking in a Democratic Society'. Paper presented at the Annual Dinner and Francis Boyer Lecture of the American Enterprise, Institute for Public Policy Research, Washington, DC, 5 December 5. https://www.federalreserve.gov/boarddocs/speeches/1996/19961205.htm (accessed 25 May 2016).

Harris, Seth, and Alan Krueger. 2015. 'A Proposal for Modernizing Labor Laws for Twenty-First-Century Work: The "Independent Worker".' The Hamilton Project. Discussion paper 2015-10. December. http://www.hamiltonproject.org/assets/files/modernizing_labor_laws_for_twenty_first_century_work_krueger_harris.pdf (accessed 25 May 2016).

Henwood, Doug. 2003. *After the New Economy*. New York: New Press.

Henwood, Doug. 2015. 'What the Sharing Economy Takes'. *The Nation*, 27 January. http://www.thenation.com/article/what-sharing-economy-takes (accessed 25 May 2016).

Herrman, John. 2016. 'Media Websites Battle Faltering Ad Revenue and Traffic'. *The New York Times*, 17 April. http://www.nytimes.com/2016/04/18/business/media-websites-battle-falteringad-revenue-and-traffic.html (accessed 30 June 2016).

Hesse, Jason. 2015. '6 per cent of Brits Use Sharing Economy to Earn Extra Cash'. Real Business. 15 September. http://realbusiness.co.uk/article/31360-6-per-cent-of-brits-use-sharing-economy-to-earn-extra-cash (accessed 25 May 2016).

Hook, Leslie. 2016. 'Amazon Leases 20 Boeing 767 Freight Jets for Air Cargo Programme'. *Financial Times*, 9 March. http://www.ft.com/cms/s/0/6f3867e8-e617-11e5-a09b-1f8b0d268c39.html (accessed 30 June 2016).

Huet, Ellen. 2016. 'Instacart Gets Red Bull and Doritos to Pay Your Delivery Fees'. Bloomberg Technology. 11 March. http://www.bloomberg.com/news/articles/2016-03-11/instacart-gets-red-bull-and-doritos-to-pay-your-delivery-fees (accessed 6 June 2016).

Huws, Ursula. 2014. *Labor in the Global Digital Economy: The Cybertariat Comes of Age*. New York: Monthly Review Press.

Huws, Ursula, and Simon Joyce. 2016. 'Crowd Working Survey'. University of Hertford-

shire. February. http://www.feps-europe.eu/
assets/a82bcd12-fb97-43a6-9346-24242695a183/
crowd-working-surveypdf.pdf (accessed 27 May
2016).

Hwang, Tim, and Madeleine Clare Elish. 2015. 'The
Mirage of the Marketplace: The Disingenuous
Ways Uber Hides behind Its Algorithm'. *Slate*,
17 July. http://www.slate.com/articles/technology/
future_tense/2015/07/uber_s_algorithm_and_
the_mirage_of_the_marketplace.single.html#lf_
comment=352895959 (accessed 27 May 2016).

International Federation of the Phonographic Industry. 2015. *IFPI Digital Music Report 2015: Charting
the Path to Sustainable Growth*. London: IFPI.
http://www.ifpi.org/downloads/Digital-Music-
Report-2015.pdf (accessed 27 May 2016).

Jones, John Philip. 1985. 'Is Total Advertising Going
Up or Down?' *International Journal of Advertising*,
4 (1): 47–64.

Jourdan, Adam, and John Ruwitch. 2016. 'Uber
Losing $1 Billion a Year to Compete in China'.
Reuters. 18 February. http://www.reuters.com/
article/uber-china-idUSKCN0VR1M9 (accessed
27 May 2016).

Joyce, Michael, Matthew Tong, and Robert Woods.
2011. 'The United Kingdom's Quantitative Easing

Policy: Design, Operation and Impact'. *Quarterly Bulletin*, Q3: 200–212.

Kamdar, Adi. 2016. 'Why Some Gig Economy Startups Are Reclassifying Workers as Employees'. On Labor: Workers, Unions, and Politics. 19 February. http://onlabor.org/2016/02/19/why-some-gig-economy-startups-are-reclassifying-workers-as-employees (accessed 27 May 2016).

Kaminska, Izabella. 2016a. 'Davos: Historians Dream of Fourth Industrial Revolutions'. *Financial Times*, 20 January. http://ftalphaville.ft.com/2016/01/20/2150720/davos-historians-dream-of-fourth-industrial-revolutions (accessed 30 June 2016).

Kaminska, Izabella. 2016b. 'On the Hypothetical Eventuality of No More Free Internet'. FT Alphaville. 10 February. http://ftalphaville.ft.com/2016/02/10/2152601/on-the-hypothetical-eventuality-of-no-more-free-internet (accessed 30 June 2016).

Kaminska, Izabella. 2016c. 'Scaling, and Why Unicorns Can't Survive Without It'. *FT Alphaville*, 15 January. http://ftalphaville.ft.com/2016/01/15/2150403/scaling-and-why-unicorns-cant-survive-without-it (accessed 30 June 2016).

Karabarbounis, Loukas, and Brent Neiman. 2012. 'Declining Labor Shares and the Global Rise of

Corporate Saving'. NBER Working Paper 18154. National Bureau of Economic Research, http://www.nber.org/papers/w18154 (accessed 27 May 2016).

Katz, Lawrence, and Alan Krueger. 2016. 'The Rise of Alternative Work Arrangements and the "Gig" Economy'. Scribd. 14 March. https://www.scribd.com/doc/306279776/Katz-and-Krueger-Alt-Work-Deck (accessed 27 May 2016).

Kawa, Luke. 2016. 'Piles of Cash Mean the Biggest Companies Will Get Even Bigger'. Bloomberg. 21 January. http://www.bloomberg.com/news/articles/2016-01-21/piles-of-cash-mean-the-biggest-companies-will-get-even-bigger (accessed 6 June, 2016).

Kelion, Leo. 2013. 'LG Investigates Smart TV "Unauthorised Spying" Claim'. BBC News. 20 November. http://www.bbc.co.uk/news/technology-25018225 (accessed 27 May 2016).

Khan, Mehreen. 2016. 'Mapped: Negative Central Bank Interest Rates Now Herald New Danger for the World'. *The Telegraph*, 15 February. http://www.telegraph.co.uk/finance/economics/12149894/Mapped-Why-negative-interest-rates-herald-new-danger-for-the-world.html (accessed 22 May 2016).

Kim, Eugene. 2016. 'Dropbox Cut a Bunch of Perks and Told Employees to Save More as Silicon Valley Startups Brace for the Cold'. Business Insider. 7 May. http://uk.businessinsider.com/cost-cutting-at-dropbox-and-silicon-valley-startups-2016-5 (accessed 22 May 2016).

Klein, Matthew. 2016. 'The US Tech Sector Is Really Small'. *Financial Times*, 8 January. http://ftalphaville.ft.com/2016/01/08/2149557/the-us-tech-sector-is-really-small (accessed 30 June 2016).

Knight, Sam. 2016. 'How Uber Conquered London'. *The Guardian*, 27 April. http://www.theguardian.com/technology/2016/apr/27/how-uber-conquered-london (accessed 22 May 2016).

Kosoff, Maya. 2015. 'Uber's Nightmare Scenario'. Business Insider. 19 July. http://uk.businessinsider.com/what-it-would-take-for-uber-to-reclassify-all-its-drivers-2015-7 (accessed 22 May 2016).

Krugman, Paul. 1998. 'It's Baaack: Japan's Slump and the Return of the Liquidity Trap'. *Brookings Papers on Economic Activity*, 29 (2): 137–206.

Kuang, Cliff. 2016. 'How Facebook's Big Bet on Chatbots Might Remake the UX of the Web'. Co.Desi.gn. 12 April. http://www.fastcodesign.com/3058818/how-facebooks-big-bet-on-chatbots-might-remake-the-ux-of-the-web (accessed 22 May 2016).

Lardinois, Frederic. 2016. 'Microsoft and Facebook Are Building the Fastest Trans-Atlantic Cable Yet'. *TechCrunch*, 26 May. https://techcrunch.com/2016/05/26/microsoft-and-facebook-are-building-the-fastest-trans-atlantic-cable-yet (accessed 30 June 2016).

Levine, Dan, and Heather Somerville. 2016. 'Uber Drivers, if Employees, Owed $730 Million More: US Court Papers'. Reuters. 10 May. http://www.reuters.com/article/us-uber-tech-drivers-lawsuit-idUSKCN0Y02E8 (accessed 22 May 2016).

Löffler, Markus, and Andreas Tschiesner. 2013. 'The Internet of Things and the Future of Manufacturing'. McKinsey & Company. http://www.mckinsey.com/insights/business_technology/the_internet_of_things_and_the_future_of_manufacturing (accessed 22 May 2016).

Manyika, James, Susan Lund, Kelsey Robinson, John Valentino, and Richard Dobbs. 2015. 'A Labor Market That Works: Connecting Talent with Opportunity in the Digital Age'. McKinsey Global Institute. http://www.mckinsey.com/global-themes/employment-and-growth/connect

ing-talent-with-opportunity-in-the-digital-age (accessed 22 May 2016).

Marx, Karl. 1990. *Capital: A Critique of Political Economy*, vol. 1, translated by Ben Fowkes. London: Penguin.

Mason, Will. 2016. 'Oculus "Always On" Services and Privacy Policy May Be a Cause for Concern'. UploadVR. 1 April. http://uploadvr.com/facebook-oculus-privacy (accessed 22 May 2016).

Maxwell, Richard, and Toby Miller. 2012. *Greening the Media*. Oxford: Oxford University Press.

McBride, Sarah, and Narottam Medhora. 2016. 'Amazon Profit Crushes Estimates as Cloud-Service Revenue Soars'. Reuters. 28 April. http://www.reuters.com/article/us-amazon-results-idUSKCN0XP2WD (accessed 22 May 2016).

McKinsey & Company. 2015. *Global Media Report, 2015: Global Industry Overview*. Global Media and Entertainment Practice. http://www.mckinsey.com/~/media/mckinsey/industries/media%20and%20entertainment/our%20insights/the%20state%20of%20global%20media%20spending/mckinsey%20global%20media%20report%202015.ashx (accessed 25 May 2016).

Meeker, Mary. 2016. *Internet Trends 2016*. Kleiner

Perkins Caufield & Byers. http://www.kpcb.com/
internet-trends (accessed 30 June 2016).

Metz, Cade. 2012. 'If Xerox PARC Invented the PC,
Google Invented the Internet'. *Wired*, 8 August.
http://www.wired.com/2012/08/google-as-xerox-
parc (accessed 22 May 2016).

Metz, Cade. 2015. 'Google Is 2 Billion Lines of Code
– And It's All in One Place'. *Wired*, 16 September.
http://www.wired.com/2015/09/google-2-billion-
lines-codeand-one-place (accessed 22 May 2016).

Miller, Ron. 2015a. 'GE Adds Infrastructure Services
to Internet of Things Platform'. TechCrunch. 4
August. http://social.techcrunch.com/2015/08/
04/ge-adds-infrastructure-services-to-internet-of-
things-platform (accessed 10 April 2016).

Miller, Ron. 2015b. 'GE Predicts Predix Platform Will
Generate $6B in Revenue This Year'. *TechCrunch*.
29 September. http://social.techcrunch.com/2015/
09/29/ge-predicts-predix-platform-will-generate-
6b-in-revenue-this-year (accessed 10 April 2016).

Miller, Ron. 2016. 'IBM Launches Quantum Computing as a Cloud Service'. TechCrunch. 3
May. http://social.techcrunch.com/2016/05/03/
ibm-brings-experimental-quantum-computing-
to-the-cloud (accessed 22 May 2016).

Mitchell, Tom. 2016. 'China Steel Overcapacity to

Remain After Restructuring'. *Financial Times*, 10 April. http://www.ft.com/cms/s/0/e62e3722-fee2-11e5-ac98-3c15a1aa2e62.html?siteedition=uk (accessed 30 June 2016).

MIT Technology Review. 2016. 'The Rise of Data Capital'. http://files.technologyreview.com/white-papers/MIT_Oracle+Report-The_Rise_of_Data_Capital.pdf (accessed 5 June 2016).

Moore, Jason W. 2015. *Capitalism in the Web of Life: Ecology and the Accumulation of Capital*. London: Verso.

Morozov, Evgeny. 2015a. 'Socialize the Data Centres!' *New Left Review*, 91: 45–66.

Morozov, Evgeny. 2015b. 'The Taming of Tech Criticism'. *The Baffler*, 27. http://thebaffler.com/salvos/taming-tech-criticism (accessed 22 May 2016).

Morozov, Evgeny. 2016. 'Tech Titans Are Busy Privatising Our Data'. *The Guardian*, 24 April. http://www.theguardian.com/commentisfree/2016/apr/24/the-new-feudalism-silicon-valley-overlords-advertising-necessary-evil (accessed 22 May 2016).

Murray, Alan. 2016. 'How GE and Henry Schein Show That Every Company Is a Tech Company'. *Fortune*, 10 June. http://fortune.com/2016/06/10/henry-schein-ge-digital-revolution (accessed 30 June 2016).

National Venture Capital Association. 2016. *Yearbook 2016*. Arlington: NVCA. http://nvca.org/?ddown load=2963 (accessed 22 May 2016).

Office for National Statistics. 2014. 'Self-Employed Workers in the UK: 2014'. Office for National Statistics, London, 20 August. http://www.ons.gov.uk/ons/dcp171776_374941.pdf (accessed 4 June 2016).

Office for National Statistics. 2016a. 'Economic Review: April 2016'. Office for National Statistics, London, 6 April. https://www.ons.gov.uk/economy/nationalaccounts/uksectoraccounts/articles/economicreview/april2016 (accessed 29 May 2016).

Office for National Statistics. 2016b. 'Employment by Industry: EMP13' (emp13may2016xls). http://www.ons.gov.uk/employmentandlabourmarket/peopleinwork/employmentandemployeetypes/datasets/employmentbyindustryemp13 (accessed 29 May 2016).

O'Keefe, Brian, and Marty Jones. 2015. 'Uber's Elaborate Tax Scheme Explained'. *Fortune*, 22 October. http://fortune.com/2015/10/22/uber-tax-shell (accessed 22 May 2016).

Pasquale, Frank. 2015. 'The Other Big Brother'. *The Atlantic*, 21 September. http://www.theatlantic.com/business/archive/2015/09/corporate-surveillance-activists/406201 (accessed 22 May 2016).

Perez, Carlota. 2009. 'The Double Bubble at the Turn of the Century: Technological Roots and Structural Implications'. *Cambridge Journal of Economics*, 33 (4): 779–805.

Piketty, Thomas. 2014. *Capital in the Twenty-First Century*, translated by Arthur Goldhammer. Cambridge, MA: Harvard University Press.

Polivka, Anne. 1996. 'Contingent and Alternative Work Arrangements, Defined'. *Monthly Labor Review*, 119 (10): 3–9.

Pollack, Lisa. 2016. 'What Is the Price for Your Personal Digital Dataset?' *Financial Times*, 10 May. http://www.ft.com/cms/s/0/1d5bd1d0-15f6-11e6-9d98–00386a18e39d.html (accessed 30 June 2016).

Rachel, Łukasz, and Thomas Smith. 2015. 'Secular Drivers of the Global Real Interest Rate'. Staff Working Paper 571. London: Bank of England. https://bankunderground.co.uk/2015/07/27/drivers-of-long-term-global-interest-rates-can-weaker-growth-explain-the-fall (accessed June 12, 2016).

'Reinventing the Deal'. 2015. *The Economist*, 24 October. http://www.economist.com/news/briefing/21676760-americas-startups-are-changing-what-it-means-own-company-reinventing-deal (accessed 4 June 2016).

Rochet, Jean-Charles, and Jean Tirole. 2003. 'Platform Competition in Two-Sided Markets'. *Journal of the European Economic Association*, 1 (4): 990–1029.

Rochet, Jean-Charles, and Jean Tirole. 2006. 'Two-Sided Markets: A Progress Report'. *The RAND Journal of Economics*, 37 (3): 645–67.

Scheiber, Noam. 2015. 'Growth in the "Gig Economy" Fuels Work Force Anxieties'. *The New York Times*, 12 July. http://www.nytimes.com/2015/07/13/business/rising-economic-insecurity-tied-to-decades-long-trend-in-employment-practices.html (accessed 4 June 2016).

Schiller, Dan. 2014. *Digital Depression: Information Technology and Economic Crisis*. Chicago, IL: University of Illinois Press.

Scholz, Trebor. 2015. *Platform Cooperativism: Challenging the Corporate Sharing Economy*. New York: Rosa Luxemburg Stiftung. http://www.rosalux-nyc.org/wp-content/files_mf/scholz_platformcooperativism_2016.pdf (accessed 4 June 2016).

Select Committee on European Union. 2016. *Online Platforms and the Digital Single Market*. London: House of Lords. http://www.publications.parliament.uk/pa/ld201516/ldselect/ldeucom/129/129.pdf (accessed 30 June 2016).

Shankland, Stephen. 2009. 'Google Uncloaks Once-Secret Server'. CNET. 11 December. http://www.cnet.com/news/google-uncloaks-once-secret-server-10209580 (accessed 4 June 2016).

Shinal, John. 2016. 'Bye-Bye Internet Bubble 2.0'. *USA Today*, 7 February. http://www.usatoday.com/story/tech/columnist/shinal/2016/02/05/bye-bye-internet-bubble-20/79887644 (accessed 4 June 2016).

Smith, Gerry. 2016. 'New York Times to Start Delivering Meal Kits to Your Home'. Bloomberg Technology. 5 May. http://www.bloomberg.com/news/articles/2016-05-05/new-york-times-to-start-delivering-meal-kits-to-your-home (accessed 4 June 2016).

Spross, Jeff. 2016. 'Rich People Have Nowhere to Put Their Money: This Is a Serious Problem'. *The Week*, 22 January. http://theweek.com/articles/600523/rich-people-have-nowhere-money-serious-problem (accessed 4 June 2016).

Srnicek, Nick, and Alex Williams. 2015. *Inventing the Future: Postcapitalism and a World without Work*. London: Verso.

Stokes, Kathleen, Emma Clarence, Lauren Anderson, and April Rinne. 2014. *Making Sense of the UK Collaborative Economy*. London: Nesta. https://www.

nesta.org.uk/sites/default/files/making_sense_of_
the_uk_collaborative_economy_14.pdf (accessed 4
June 2016).

Stucke, Maurice, and Allen Grunes. 2016. *Big Data
and Competition Policy*. Oxford: Oxford University Press.

Taylor, Edward. 2016. 'Amazon, Microsoft Look
for Big Data Role in Self-Driving Cars'. *Reuters*, 1 April. http://www.reuters.com/article/
us-automakers-here-amazon-idUSKCN0WX2D8
(accessed 4 June 2016).

Terranova, Tiziana. 2000. 'Free Labor: Producing
Culture for the Digital Economy'. *Social Text*, 18
(2.63): 33–58.

US Department of Labor. 2005. 'Contingent and
Alternative Employment Arrangements, February
2005'. News. Bureau of Labor Statistics, Washington, DC. http://www.bls.gov/news.release/pdf/
conemp.pdf (accessed 4 June 2016).

US Department of Labor. 2016a. 'Databases, Tables
and Calculators by Subject: Output'. Bureau of
Labor Statistics, Washington, DC. http://data.
bls.gov/timeseries/PRS30006042 (accessed 9 June,
2016).

US Department of Labor. 2016b. 'Databases, Tables
and Calculators by Subject: Output: Labor

Productivity'. Bureau of Labor Statistics, Washington, DC. http://data.bls.gov/timeseries/PRS3000 6042 (accessed 9 June, 2016).

US Department of Labor, n.d. 'Press Releases: Employee Misclassification as Independent Contractors'. Wage and Hour Division (WHD). http://www.dol.gov/whd/workers/misclassifica tion/pressrelease.htm (accessed 12 June, 2016).

US Energy Information Administration. n.d. 'International Energy Statistics: Electricity Consumption'. https://www.eia.gov/cfapps/ipdbproject/iedin dex3.cfm?tid=2&pid=2&aid=2&cid=regions& syid=2012&eyid=2012&unit=BKWH (accessed 12 May 2016).

van der Wurff, Richard, Piet Bakker, and Robert Picard. 2008. 'Economic Growth and Advertising Expenditures in Different Media in Different Countries'. *Journal of Media Economics*, 21 (1): 28–52.

Varian, Hal. 2009. 'Online Ad Auctions'. *American Economic Review*, 99 (2): 430–34.

Varian, Hal. 2015. 'Big Data and Economic Measurement'. Paper presented at the Stockholm School of Economics, Stockholm External Seminar, 7 September. https://soundcloud.com/snsinfo/2015-09-08-sns-sifr-finanspanel-googles-chefekonom-hal-varian (accessed June 10, 2016).

Vega, Tanzina, and Stuart Elliott. 2011. 'After Two Slow Years, an Industry Rebound Begins'. *The New York Times*, 2 January. http://www.nytimes.com/2011/01/03/business/media/03adco.html (accessed 29 May 2016).

Vercellone, Carlo. 2007. 'From Formal Subsumption to General Intellect: Elements for a Marxist Reading of the Thesis of Cognitive Capitalism'. *Historical Materialism*, 15 (1): 13–36.

Wark, McKenzie. 2004. *A Hacker Manifesto*. Cambridge, MA: Harvard University Press.

Waters, Richard. 2016. 'Microsoft's Nadella Taps Potential of Industrial Internet of Things'. *Financial Times*, 22 April. http://www.ft.com/cms/s/0/c8e2e1d0-0861-11e6-a623-b84d06a39ec2.html (accessed 30 June 2016).

Webb, Alex. 2015. 'Can Germany Beat the US to the Industrial Internet?' Bloomberg Businessweek, 18 September. http://www.bloomberg.com/news/articles/2015-09-18/can-the-mittelstand-fend-off-u-s-software-giants- (accessed 29 May 2016).

Wheelock, Jane. 1983. 'Competition in the Marxist Tradition'. *Capital & Class*, 7 (3): 18–47.

Wile, Rob. 2016. 'There Are Probably Way More People in the "Gig Economy" Than We Realize'. *Fusion*. Accessed 24 March. http://fusion.net/

story/173244/there-are-probably-way-more-peo
ple-in-the-gig-economy-than-we-realize (accessed
29 May 2016).

Wittel, Andreas. 2016. 'Digital Marx: Toward a Political Economy of Distributed Media'. In *Marx in
the Age of Digital Capitalism*, edited by Christian
Fuchs and Vincent Mosco, pp. 68–104. Leiden:
Brill.

World Bank. 2016. 'World Development Reports,
2016: Digital Dividends'. Washington, DC. http://
www.worldbank.org/en/publication/wdr2016
(accessed 29 May 2016).

World Economic Forum. 2015. 'Industrial Internet
of Things: Unleashing the Potential of Connected
Products and Services'. New York. http://www3.
weforum.org/docs/WEFUSA_IndustrialInternet_
Report2015.pdf (accessed 27 May 2016).

World Steel Association. 2016. 'March 2016 Crude
Steel Production'. Brussels. http://www.worldsteel.
org/statistics/crude-steel-production-2016-2015.
html (accessed 29 May 2016).

WordStream. 2011. 'What Industries Contributed
the Most to Google's Earnings?' WordStream
Inc. http://www.wordstream.com/articles/google-
earnings (accessed 29 May 2016).

Zaske, Sara. 2015. 'Germany's Vision for Industrie

4.0: The Revolution Will Be Digitised'. *ZDNet*, 23 February. http://www.zdnet.com/article/ger manys-vision-for-industrie-4-0-the-revolution-will-be-digitised (accessed 10 June 2016).

Zuboff, Shoshana. 2015. 'Big Other: Surveillance Capitalism and the Prospects of an Information Civilization'. *Journal of Information Technology*, 30 (1): 75–89. doi: 10.1057/jit.2015.5.

Zuboff, Shoshana. 2016. 'Google as a Fortune Teller: The Secrets of Surveillance Capitalism'. *Frankfurter Allgemeine Zeitung*, 5 March. http://www.faz.net/ aktuell/feuilleton/debatten/the-digital-debate/ shoshana-zuboff-secrets-of-surveillance-capital ism-14103616.html (accessed 12 June 2016).

Zucman, Gabriel. 2015. *The Hidden Wealth of Nations: The Scourge of Tax Havens*, translated by Teresa Lavender Fagan. Chicago, IL: University of Chicago Press.